The Hamlyn
CHICKEN
COOKBOOK

The Hamlyn
CHICKEN
COOKBOOK

Elizabeth Pomeroy

Hamlyn
London · New York · Sydney · Toronto

The author and publishers would like to thank the following for their
help in supplying colour photographs for this book:
British Chicken Limited, pages 33, 51, 52, 86 and 103
Cover photographs by Paul Williams

First published 1973 under the title *Chicken Cookbook*

This completely revised and updated edition
published 1981 by
The Hamlyn Publishing Group Limited
London · New York · Sydney · Toronto
Astronaut House, Feltham, Middlesex, England
© Copyright The Hamlyn Publishing Group Limited 1980

Reprinted 1983

ISBN 0 600 32233 5

Phototypeset by Photocomp Limited, Birmingham
Printed in Italy

Contents

Useful facts and figures

Notes on metrication

In this book quantities are given in metric and Imperial measures. Exact conversion from Imperial to metric measures does not usually give very convenient working quantities and so the metric measures have been rounded off into units of 25 grams. The table below shows the recommended equivalents.

Ounces	Approx g to nearest whole figure	Recommended conversion to nearest unit of 25	Ounces	Approx g to nearest whole figure	Recommended conversion to nearest unit of 25
1	28	25	11	312	300
2	57	50	12	340	350
3	85	75	13	368	375
4	113	100	14	396	400
5	142	150	15	425	425
6	170	175	16 (1 lb)	454	450
7	198	200	17	482	475
8	227	225	18	510	500
9	255	250	19	539	550
10	283	275	20 ($1\frac{1}{4}$ lb)	567	575

Note When converting quantities over 20 oz first add the appropriate figures in the centre column, then adjust to the nearest unit of 25. As a general guide, 1 kg (1000 g) equals 2·2 lb or about 2 lb 3 oz. This method of conversion gives good results in nearly all cases, although in certain pastry and cake recipes a more accurate conversion is necessary to produce a balanced recipe.

Liquid measures The millilitre has been used in this book and the following table gives a few examples.

Imperial	Approx ml to nearest whole figure	Recommended ml	Imperial	Approx ml to nearest whole figure	Recommended ml
$\frac{1}{4}$ pint	142	150 ml	1 pint	567	600 ml
$\frac{1}{2}$ pint	283	300 ml	$1\frac{1}{2}$ pints	851	900 ml
$\frac{3}{4}$ pint	425	450 ml	$1\frac{3}{4}$ pints	992	1000 ml (1 litre)

Spoon measures All spoon measures given in this book are level unless otherwise stated.

Can sizes At present, cans are marked with the exact (usually to the nearest whole number) metric equivalent of the Imperial weight of the contents, so we have followed this practice when giving can sizes.

Oven temperatures

The table below gives recommended equivalents.

	°C	°F	Gas Mark		°C	°F	Gas Mark
Very cool	110	225	$\frac{1}{4}$	Moderately hot	190	375	5
	120	250	$\frac{1}{2}$		200	400	6
Cool	140	275	1	Hot	220	425	7
	150	300	2		230	450	8
Moderate	160	325	3	Very hot	240	475	9
	180	350	4				

Notes for American and Australian users

In America the 8-oz measuring cup is used. In Australia metric measures are now used in conjunction with the standard 250-ml measuring cup. The Imperial pint, used in Britain and Australia, is 20 fl oz, while the American pint is 16 fl oz. It is important to remember that the Australian tablespoon differs from both the British and American tablespoons; the table below gives a comparison. The British standard tablespoon, which has been used throughout this book, holds 17·7 ml, the American 14·2 ml, and the Australian 20 ml. A teaspoon holds approximately 5 ml in all three countries.

British	American	Australian	British	American	Australian
1 teaspoon	1 teaspoon	1 teaspoon	3½ table-spoons	4 table-spoons	3 table-spoons
1 table-spoon	1 table-spoon	1 table-spoon	4 table-spoons	5 table-spoons	3½ table-spoons
2 table-spoons	3 table-spoons	2 table-spoons			

An Imperial/American guide to solid and liquid measures

Imperial	American	Imperial	American
Solid measures		**Liquid measures**	
1 lb butter or margarine	2 cups	$\frac{1}{4}$ pint liquid	$\frac{2}{3}$ cup liquid
		$\frac{1}{2}$ pint	1$\frac{1}{4}$ cups
1 lb flour	4 cups	$\frac{3}{4}$ pint	2 cups
1 lb granulated or castor sugar	2 cups	1 pint	2$\frac{1}{2}$ cups
		1$\frac{1}{2}$ pints	3$\frac{3}{4}$ cups
1 lb icing sugar	3 cups	2 pints	5 cups (2$\frac{1}{2}$ pints)
8 oz rice	1 cup		

Note: When making any of the recipes in this book, only follow one set of measures as they are not interchangeable.

Introduction

There are so many delicious and diverse ways of cooking chicken that I found it very difficult to decide which to choose for this book.

What I have tried to do is, firstly, to help the beginner home cook with basic information and enjoyable uncomplicated recipes to overcome any initial lack of confidence and to embark on shopping and cooking with positive pleasure, instead of anxiety. Next, to encourage the more experienced cook/host and hostess to enliven their menus with some dashing new dishes which they will enjoy preparing and the guests have pleasure in eating. Incidentally, if you are calorie counting, grilled or roast chicken provides one of the most appetising meals for slimmers.

There are many home cooks for whom the demands of a job outside the home and/or a lively family inside it, present a time problem; for them I have included a number of family and party dishes, which can be prepared in advance and finished off in a short time when required.

Today, when the cost of rearing most farm animals is continually rising, chicken production, which is a rapid process so less vulnerable to shortages than other meat, keeps poultry prices well within reach of the average family. As a result, chicken is now regularly included on many shopping lists and some of us may be tempted to fall into the trap of repeating familiar chicken dishes just because we can toss them off and no-one complains. Let us be adventurous and look abroad for fresh ideas – it is surprising how many of the exotic and exciting dishes are easy to make!

Elizabeth Pomeroy

Buying birds

The marketing scene for poultry has changed remarkably during recent years. As a result of intensive production methods, the shopper is now offered what is, to some, a bewildering choice of birds of varying sizes and presumably ages: also half chickens, quarter chickens, chicken breasts and wings and legs. The labels may read 'free range' or 'farm fresh', 'pre-packed fresh' or 'frozen', so perhaps we had better start here.

Free range should only be applied to birds which have spent their lives pecking about out of doors in a farmyard or orchard. They, alas, are now definitely a minority group.

Farm fresh means that although the birds have been reared under modern methods, they come fresh, usually plucked, from the producers to the poulterer, who draws and trusses them for the customers. They have a chance to hang for a day or so, which much improves their flavour.

Pre-packed fresh means that the birds have been dressed by the producer, then chilled and packed in transparent film without being frozen.

Frozen means they have been killed, plucked, drawn and frozen at rapid factory speed and then stored at a freezing temperature for varying periods, first by the producer and then the retailer, until bought by the customer. These birds, when whole, are best if allowed to thaw out in the refrigerator or cold larder for 24 hours before cooking. This slightly compensates for the lack of hanging prior to processing and it ensures that the bird is completely thawed out before cooking, which is absolutely essential.

How do I choose for quality?

For roasting, grilling and frying you want a young, tender bird, as plump as possible. Free range or farm fresh will have more flavour than a frozen bird. The latter are less expensive and, with the support of an interesting or exciting sauce, make a tasty dish. To test if a bird is young, bend the rear end of the breastbone – in a young, tender bird this is pliable gristle, while in an old bird it becomes rigid.

For boiling and casseroling a more mature bird may be used as it can be tenderised by long cooking at a low temperature. Boilers (not to be confused with 'broilers' which are young birds for grilling and frying) are much the cheapest. They used to be aged barnyard fowls needing half a day to cook, but nowadays, because of intensive egg production, many laying hens are killed off when only a year old and after $2\frac{1}{2}$–3 hours boiling will make many delectable dishes. The younger birds have an amount of yellow fat which can be skimmed off the stock after boiling and used to add flavour to other chicken dishes such as risotto.

9

Buying chart

Bird	Age	Dressed weight	Portions	Suitable cooking method
Baby chickens (poussins)	4–6 weeks	0·5 kg/1 lb	1–2	Spit or oven roast Split and grill or fry
Spring chickens	6–10 weeks	0·75–1 kg/ 1½–2 lb	2	Spit or oven roast Split and grill or fry
Broilers	3–4 months	1–1·25 kg/ 2–2½ lb	3–4	Spit or oven roast Joint and grill or fry
Roasters	6–12 months	1·5–1·75 kg/ 3–4 lb	4–5	Spit or oven roast Joint and sauté
Capons	6–12 months	2·25–3·5 kg/ 5–8 lb	6–8	Oven roast
Boilers	1 year plus	2–2·75 kg/ 4½–6 lb	4–6	Simmer very slowly

NOTE: Any of these birds can be pot-roasted or casseroled, see recipes.

How do I select for size?

Pre-packed and frozen chickens are sold by oven-ready weight, that is, already drawn and with head and feet removed. Chilled and frozen birds are sometimes sold without giblets, so watch out if you want to make giblet stock or chicken liver stuffing. Allow about 275 g/10 oz chicken per head oven-ready weight or a 1·25–1·5-kg/2½–3-lb roasting bird for four people.

Free range and farm fresh birds are also sometimes sold ready trussed, but often they are only plucked and then hung in the poulterers. They are weighed and priced before drawing and lose about 40 per cent of their weight when drawn and with head and feet removed, so allow 0·5 kg/1 lb of chicken per person, undressed weight.

10

If buying a roasting chicken for six people, a 2·75-kg/6-lb capon would carve into six good portions. These are neutered cockerels which, being greedy and lazy, become beautifully plump and tender. (In France they also caponise hens, which are then called *poulardes*.) These large birds, weighing from 2·25–3·5 kg/ 5–8 lb, are expensive to rear and this is reflected in the price, but the flesh is of particularly high quality. For eight people, a more economical buy would be two smaller birds weighing 1·25–1·5 kg/2½–3 lb each.

When are chicken joints a good buy?

These are sold fresh and frozen and are very useful if you want to make a dish like Chicken Kiev, in which only the breasts are used and you do not want any chicken left over. For four helpings, it is more economical to buy a whole bird and it is less expensive than four joints, and the carcass and giblets will give you a useful stock. If you have time and a freezer, it is a good opportunity to make the dark meat into a casserole or other dish and freeze it for future use.

Chickens are also sold in 'quarters' and this means the bird is chopped across into four, not jointed, so the breast is halved (and cannot be stuffed) and the rib-cage and thick backbone are still attached. It is a good idea to cut these bones off to make a little stock for gravy or a base for an interesting sauce to serve with the chicken.

Drumsticks are a convenient and economical buy for Chicken in a basket (page 23), and boned fillets are now available which are excellent for elegant sauté dishes.

Why must poultry be completely thawed before cooking?

Harmful bacteria tend to lurk near the bone and if the flesh around it is still frozen when the bird is put on to cook, the heat may not penetrate fully to the bone and in the semi-warmth the bacteria multiply instead of being rendered harmless by high temperature. Cut chicken portions take less time to thaw than a whole bird, but equal care must be taken to make sure they are completely thawed before grilling or frying, as they could brown on the outside and look appetising, while being only partially cooked inside.

How do I store poultry?

Fresh poultry should be hung, before drawing, by the feet in a cool, airy place and will keep perfectly like this for 2 or 3 days. Once drawn, it should be refrigerated and will keep for 2 or 3 days more. The giblets, however, should be cooked as soon as possible and refrigerated in their broth.

Frozen poultry can be stored in the freezer for several months and should be thawed out carefully before cooking, as explained above.

Birds in the oven and on the spit

Oven roasting

There are two methods of oven roasting – the fast method at high temperature in a moderately hot oven (200°C, 400°F, Gas Mark 6) favoured in England, and the slow method at a lower temperature in a moderate oven (180°C, 350°F, Gas Mark 4) preferred in the U.S.A.

In France and other Continental countries, poultry is cooked in a hot oven, but stock is put in the roasting pan. This gradually evaporates, producing steam, which reduces shrinkage and keeps the bird moist. It is also basted with a buttery stock during cooking which gives it a good colour.

Covered roasting pans are used by some housewives who find them easier to clean than the oven interior, but the bird will have a similar texture to one which has been pot-roasted on top of the stove. Happily ovens are now being designed with self-cleaning linings, which is a welcome progress.

Roasting in aluminium foil will prevent oven-splashing and reduce shrinkage; but except for a large bird like turkey, which is in the oven for 2–3 hours, the foil needs to be opened for the last 20 minutes despite probable splashing, if you want a crisp brown finish.

Roasting bags of transparent film allow the bird to brown during cooking and are excellent for cooking chicken joints, but a whole bird will not have quite the same texture as one that has been basted.

Cooking fats suitable for roasting poultry are lard, vegetable fats, unsalted or clarified butter and dripping from the same type of bird; that is, do not mix duck, goose, turkey or game fat with chicken dripping because of the distinctive flavours. Chicken, turkey, guinea fowl and pheasant do not have a layer of fat under the skin as do duck and goose, so the breast must be protected during roasting by a covering of pork or bacon fat and well-buttered greaseproof paper, or by frequent basting if the flesh is not to become too dry.

To stuff a chicken

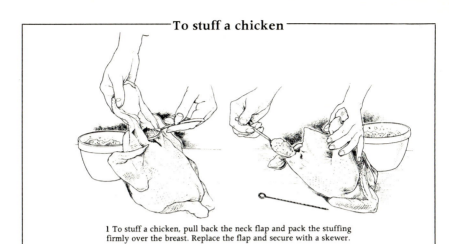

1 To stuff a chicken, pull back the neck flap and pack the stuffing firmly over the breast. Replace the flap and secure with a skewer.

2 Spoon the remaining stuffing into the body through the vent at the rear of the bird and secure with a skewer.

To truss a chicken

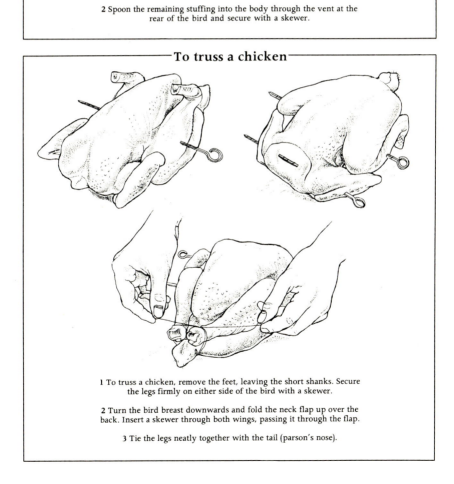

1 To truss a chicken, remove the feet, leaving the short shanks. Secure the legs firmly on either side of the bird with a skewer.

2 Turn the bird breast downwards and fold the neck flap up over the back. Insert a skewer through both wings, passing it through the flap.

3 Tie the legs neatly together with the tail (parson's nose).

Roast farmhouse chicken
(English style)
(Illustrated on page 33)

METRIC/IMPERIAL	AMERICAN
1 (1·5–2-kg/3½–4-lb) roasting chicken	1 (3½–4-lb) roaster chicken
Rice and watercress stuffing (page 120)	Rice and watercress stuffing (page 120)
2–3 tablespoons chicken dripping, unsalted butter or lard	3–4 tablespoons chicken dripping, sweet butter or lard
100 g/4 oz streaky bacon rashers	¼ lb bacon slices
watercress to garnish	watercress to garnish
giblet stock:	*giblet stock:*
1 small onion, peeled	1 small onion, peeled
1 sprig each thyme and parsley	1 sprig each thyme and parsley
1 bay leaf	1 bay leaf
salt and freshly ground black pepper	salt and freshly ground black pepper

Clean the giblets (page 54), put into a saucepan of cold water with the onion, herbs and seasoning, cover and simmer gently until the stock is required.

Prepare the rice and watercress stuffing according to the recipe, fill the breast of the chicken and truss neatly.Place the bird in a well-greased roasting pan. Remove the rind and any gristle from the bacon and cover the breast. Spread the fat over the legs and cover the bird with fatted greaseproof paper or foil. Roast in a moderately hot oven (200°C, 400°F, Gas Mark 6) for 1 hour, then remove the paper or foil and set the crisp bacon rashers aside and keep warm. Baste the chicken with the fat in the pan and return it to the oven for a further 15 minutes to brown the breast.

To test when the bird is ready, insert a skewer into the leg and press out a little of the juice – it will be amber-coloured when cooked.

Remove the chicken to a heated carving dish and keep warm. Slowly pour the fat out of a corner of the roasting pan, leaving the residue and juices in the bottom. Add 300–450 ml/½–¾ pint (U.S. 1¼–2 cups) giblet stock to the pan and boil briskly to reduce it, scraping the residue up from the bottom. When the gravy is a nice colour, season to taste and pour it into a warm sauce boat.

Arrange the crisped bacon rashers round the bird and garnish with fresh watercress sprigs. Serve with the gravy and Bread sauce (page 95). Accompany the roast chicken with roast or jacket potatoes and cauliflower or leeks. To make larger or more portions, bake pork chipolata sausages in the oven for the last 20 minutes of the cooking time and arrange around the serving dish with the bacon. *Serves 4–5*

Roast tarragon chicken
(French style)

METRIC/IMPERIAL	AMERICAN
1 (1·5-kg/3½-lb) roasting chicken	1 (3½-lb) roaster chicken
50 g/2 oz butter	¼ cup butter
2 tablespoons chopped fresh tarragon or 2 teaspoons dried tarragon	3 tablespoons chopped fresh tarragon or 2 teaspoons dried tarragon
1 small clove garlic	1 small clove garlic
salt and freshly ground black pepper	salt and freshly ground black pepper
300 ml/½ pint Giblet stock (page 54)	1¼ cups Giblet stock (page 54)
2 tablespoons brandy or sherry	3 tablespoons brandy or sherry
4 tablespoons double cream	⅓ cup heavy cream

Truss the chicken neatly (page 13). Cream together the butter and tarragon. Crush the garlic and blend into the butter. Season to taste with salt and pepper. Spread some of the tarragon butter over the bird and put the rest inside.

Place the bird on its side on a grid in the roasting pan. Pour in the stock and cook in a moderately hot oven (200°C, 400°F, Gas Mark 6) for 20 minutes. Turn the bird on to the other side, baste and roast for another 20 minutes. Turn the chicken breast upwards and baste again. Continue roasting for a further 20 minutes or until the juice runs amber-coloured when the thigh is pierced with a skewer.

Place the chicken on a heated serving dish and keep warm.

Remove the grid from the roasting pan. Pour off the fat, retaining the juices. Add the brandy or sherry, boil and then stir in the cream.

Season and pour into a warmed sauce boat.

Serve with potato croquettes, Courgettes au gratin (page 123) or casseroled green peas. *Serves 4*

To carve roast chicken

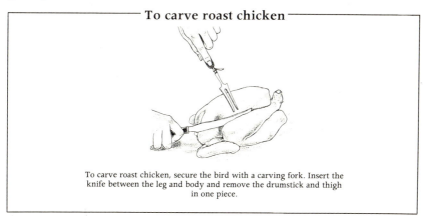

To carve roast chicken, secure the bird with a carving fork. Insert the knife between the leg and body and remove the drumstick and thigh in one piece.

Spit-roasting

This is particularly suitable for the smaller birds, chicken and game from 0·5–1·5 kg/1–3 lb. The bird must be very neatly trussed (page 13) and the spit passed through it so that the weight is evenly distributed, or the bird will slip while revolving. As the flesh shrinks during cooking, the prongs of the fork at each end of the spit may need adjusting to hold the bird secure.

The grill should be well heated and the bird basted with oil before cooking is started. Once the bird is golden brown, the heat may be slightly reduced. Frequent basting improves the texture and a sprig of thyme, rosemary or tarragon and a knob of butter inside the bird enhance the flavour. Cooking times are similar to those for oven roasting and gravies can be made in the same way.

Barbecued chicken

Chicken is ideal for spit-roasting out of doors over a charcoal brazier.

The bed of charcoal should be shallow so that it is easy to control, and built up slightly behind the spit, with the heat adjustable either by regulating the draught or by raising or lowering the spit. Do not poke the charcoal because this will slow down the fire, not brighten it.

It is important not to start cooking until the flames have died down and the charcoal has been raked over. It should be ash grey by daylight and have a soft red glow by night.

The chicken should be well oiled and dusted liberally with paprika to give it a rosy flush. Alternatively, baste the chicken frequently with a well-seasoned marinade of soured cream (page 99) or oil and lemon juice flavoured with finely chopped herbs and onions or with a spicy Barbecue sauce (page 96).

If cooking more than one chicken at a time, push the birds closely together, head to tail, between the spit forks.

Carve the chicken and serve with Apricot and honey barbecue sauce (page 97), or Tartare sauce (page 100). Accompany with baked jacket potatoes, sweet corn or roasted sweet peppers and foil-baked peas and beans, or hot French garlic bread (page 123) and bowls of cucumber and tomato salad and tossed green salad with French dressing.

Alternative methods: If it is more convenient, the chicken may be spit-roasted on a rotisserie. Baste with a barbecue sauce for the last 30 minutes.

Alternatively, the bird may be jointed (page 65) and baked in a moderately hot oven (200°C, 400°F, Gas Mark 6) for about 45 minutes. If you use this method, baste the bird with a barbecue sauce (page 96) while cooking (illustrated on page 103).

Bird under the grill

Cooking under the grill is the quickest and simplest method of all, but the meat must be tender and the joints small – poussins and spring chickens should be split in half and pressed flat and broilers divided into four or six joints (page 65).
a) To keep the chicken juicy, brush with oil, melted butter, plain or savoury, or with a marinade (page 99) or a spicy sauce which contains butter, cream or oil.
b) Heat the grill and grease the grid to prevent sticking.
c) Arrange the bird on the grid so that it is about 10 cm/4 inches below the flame.
d) Grill the first side until crispy brown but not charred. Turn, brush and grill the second side. If the chicken is thick and requires further cooking, lower the heat slightly and grill for another 5–10 minutes, turning as required. If in doubt, test with a skewer in the thickest part, the juice should be amber-coloured.

Devilled chicken legs

Raw or cooked, chicken will be more tasty if marinated in a sauce for some time prior to cooking. If the legs are from a cooked bird, make some slashes across or down them so the sauce can penetrate and prevent dryness.

METRIC/IMPERIAL	AMERICAN
2 chicken legs	2 chicken legs
White or Dark devil sauce	White or Dark devil sauce
(page 98 or 99)	(page 98 or 99)
4–6 large flat mushrooms	4–6 large flat mushrooms
salt and freshly ground	salt and freshly ground
black pepper	black pepper
40 g/1½ oz butter	3 tablespoons butter
2 large tomatoes, halved	2 large tomatoes, halved
sugar	sugar
4 rashers streaky bacon or	4 bacon slices or 2 small
2 sausages	sausages

Slash the chicken legs, cover with the devil sauce and leave to marinate.
   Wash or peel the mushrooms and remove the stalks. Season the dark side and dot with butter. Season the tomatoes with sugar, salt and pepper.
   Remove the bacon rind, roll neatly and thread on to a skewer. Heat the grill and cook the chicken legs on the first side as explained previously. Turn and coat with more sauce. Arrange on the grid the tomatoes and mushrooms, seasoned side uppermost, and the bacon rolls or sausages – turn the bacon or sausages frequently so they brown evenly. Remove the vegetables as soon as ready and, if necessary, lower the heat and cook the meat longer. Serve immediately, pouring over the sauce. *Serves 2*

Spatchcock poussins

METRIC/IMPERIAL	AMERICAN
2 poussins	2 small broiler chickens
75 g/3 oz softened butter	6 tablespoons softened butter
grated rind of $\frac{1}{2}$ lemon	grated rind of $\frac{1}{2}$ lemon
1 teaspoon crushed rosemary	1 teaspoon crushed rosemary
1 clove garlic (optional)	1 clove garlic (optional)
salt and freshly ground	salt and freshly ground
black pepper	black pepper
6 tablespoons white wine	$\frac{1}{2}$ cup white wine
4 tablespoons cream	$\frac{1}{3}$ cup cream
chopped parsley to garnish	chopped parsley to garnish

Split and truss the chicks spatchcock style (see below).

Cream the butter with the lemon rind, herbs, garlic and seasoning and spread generously over the fleshy side of the bird. Heat the grill, arrange the birds on the greased grid and cook the first side until golden brown. Turn, spread with more savoury butter and grill the other side.

Lower the heat and continue grilling about 5 minutes more on each side until tender. Remove each chick to a heated serving dish and keep warm.

Remove the grid from the grill pan, pour in the wine and boil to reduce, scraping up the juices from the base of the pan. Stir in the cream, adjust the seasoning and pour over the chicks. Sprinkle with freshly chopped parsley and serve at once.

Accompany with sauté potatoes and buttered spinach, peas or green beans.
Serves 2

Spatchcock poussins

1 Place the chicken breast upwards and cut down the centre only with poultry shears or a sharp knife, just enough to enable the breastbone to be removed. Remove the breastbone and flatten the bird with a cutlet bat or rolling pin.

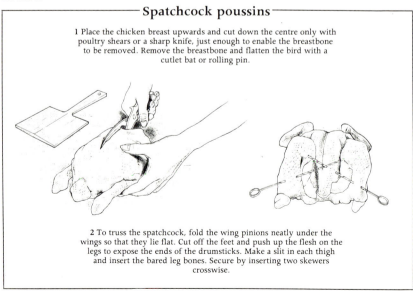

2 To truss the spatchcock, fold the wing pinions neatly under the wings so that they lie flat. Cut off the feet and push up the flesh on the legs to expose the ends of the drumsticks. Make a slit in each thigh and insert the bared leg bones. Secure by inserting two skewers crosswise.

Bird in the frying pan

Shallow frying

This is a quick and successful way of cooking chicken breasts, fillets of turkey white meat and spatchcocked small birds such as poussins.

Suitable fats are lard, clarified and unsalted butter. Butter gives an excellent flavour, but as it tends to darken quickly, it is advisable to dilute it with a tasteless oil such as corn oil, or with olive oil if you like a Mediterranean flavour.

Spatchcocked spring chicken
(Italian style)

This dish is best cooked in a shallow flameproof casserole or a skillet, that is, a frying pan with a lid. A spring chicken or two poussins are ideal for two persons.

METRIC/IMPERIAL	AMERICAN
1 spring chicken or 2 poussins	1 large or 2 small broiler chickens
seasoned flour for coating	seasoned flour for coating
25 g/1 oz butter	2 tablespoons butter
1 tablespoon olive oil	1 tablespoon olive oil
1 medium onion, sliced	1 medium onion, sliced
50 g/2 oz mushrooms	½ cup mushrooms
1½ tablespoons sherry	2 tablespoons sherry
1 (227-g/8-oz) can tomatoes	1 (8-oz) can tomatoes
1 sprig basil or marjoram	1 sprig basil or marjoram
salt and freshly ground black pepper	salt and freshly ground black pepper
lemon juice to taste	lemon juice to taste

Truss the chicken spatchcock style (opposite) and coat with seasoned flour, patting off any surplus.

Heat the butter and oil and fry the chicken until nicely browned, turning once. Remove from the pan and fry the onion gently until softened. Wash the mushrooms and halve if large. Add these to the pan and continue frying until the onion starts to colour. Pour in the sherry and boil up. Stir in the tomatoes and herbs, season and add lemon juice to taste. Add the chicken, cover and simmer gently for 20 minutes, or until tender.

Serve with buttered pasta and Spinach croquettes (page 124). *Serves 2*

Chicken breasts with apricots and brandy

This is a delightful dish for a *diner à deux*. The breasts from a 1·5-kg/3½-lb bird will weigh about 100 g/4 oz each and one per portion will be sufficient. If using smaller birds, two may be required.

METRIC/IMPERIAL	AMERICAN
50 g/2 oz dried apricots	⅓ cup dried apricots
2–4 chicken breasts	2–4 chicken breasts
seasoned flour for coating	seasoned flour for coating
25 g/1 oz unsalted butter	2 tablespoons sweet butter
1 tablespoon vegetable oil	1 tablespoon vegetable oil
2 tablespoons brandy	3 tablespoons brandy
2–3 tablespoons soured cream	3–4 tablespoons dairy sour cream
lemon juice to taste	lemon juice to taste
salt and freshly ground	salt and freshly ground
black pepper	black pepper
toasted flaked almonds or	toasted flaked almonds or
chopped walnuts to garnish	chopped walnuts to garnish

The apricots can be plumped by soaking overnight, alternatively put into a saucepan with cold water to cover, heat gradually and simmer gently for 10 minutes until partially cooked–they are best slightly undercooked or they will go mushy in the sauce.

Fillet the chicken breasts carefully away from the bone, removing the pinions. Put between sheets of greaseproof paper and beat out flat so they resemble veal escalopes. Coat in seasoned flour, rubbing it in well. Heat the butter and oil in a frying pan and fry the breasts briskly until golden brown, turning once. Lower the heat. Drain the apricots, setting the liquid aside, and add to the pan.

Warm the brandy in a soup ladle or tiny saucepan, set it alight and pour it flaming over the chicken. Shake the pan until the flames die down. Mix 150 ml/¼ pint (U. S. ⅔ cup) of the apricot liquor into the cream and stir this into the pan. Season to taste and simmer for 5 minutes or until the chicken is tender. Add extra apricot liquor if there is not quite enough sauce.

Serve at once in a border of fluffy boiled rice or buttered noodles. Sprinkle the chicken with toasted flaked almonds or chopped walnuts.

Accompany with Courgettes au gratin (page 123) or buttered French beans.
Serves 2

Variations: Double cream sharpened with lemon juice may be used instead of soured cream.

Whisky may be used instead of brandy.

Deep frying

Chicken quarters or joints are easier to cook successfully in deep fat, rather than in a shallow frying pan. The chicken pieces should always be coated in egg and breadcrumbs or batter to prevent the juices from seeping out. The heat of the fat must be carefully controlled so that the outside of the joints are crisp, whilst the chicken is cooked right through to the centre.

Chicken Kiev

This recipe uses only the breasts and wings of each bird; provision should be made for using up the rest in casseroles, pies or rice dishes.

Chicken Kiev requires careful preparation, but it can be kept overnight in the refrigerator before frying or be deep frozen for future use.

METRIC/IMPERIAL	AMERICAN
2 (1–1·5-kg/2½–3-lb) roasting chickens	2 (2½–3-lb) roaster chickens
100 g/4 oz softened unsalted butter	½ cup softened sweet butter
grated rind and juice of 1 lemon	grated rind and juice of 1 lemon
1½ tablespoons chopped parsley	2 tablespoons chopped parsley
1 teaspoon tarragon or rosemary	1 teaspoon tarragon or rosemary
pinch of grated nutmeg or ground mace	dash of grated nutmeg or ground mace
salt and freshly ground black pepper	salt and freshly ground black pepper
seasoned flour for coating	seasoned flour for coating
1 egg	1 egg
fresh breadcrumbs for coating	fresh soft bread crumbs for coating
deep fat for frying	deep fat for frying
parsley and lemon wedges to garnish	parsley and lemon wedges to garnish

Carefully fillet the two sides of the breast of each chicken leaving the wing bone attached and beat flat.

Cream together the butter, lemon rind and herbs and flavour to taste with lemon juice, spice and seasoning. Shape into a rectangle and chill until hard. Cut into four pieces, lay one on each chicken breast then fold up neatly, pressing well together. Secure with wooden cocktail sticks. Roll in seasoned flour and pat off any surplus. Coat with beaten egg and crumbs. Coat a second time for a perfect finish. Chill well before frying – leave overnight if preferred.

Heat the deep fat to 190–195°C/375–380°F, put the chicken into the greased frying basket and cook until golden brown (page 22). Drain on soft paper, remove the sticks and put a cutlet frill on the wing bone. Serve immediately. Garnish with lemon wedges and parsley.

Serve with French fried or soufflé potatoes and a tossed green salad. *Serves 4*

Maryland chicken

(Illustrated on page 86)

This traditional dish from the Southern States of America is a firm favourite on both sides of the Atlantic. A small, tender chicken should be chosen, as long frying tends to darken the golden coating. The electric frying pan is an excellent ally, because the temperature is so easily controlled, but any deep, thick frying pan will do.

METRIC/IMPERIAL	AMERICAN
1 (1–1·25-kg/2–2½-lb) roasting chicken	1 (2–2½-lb) roaster chicken
50 g/2 oz seasoned flour	½ cup seasoned flour
1 egg	1 egg
1 tablespoon water	1 tablespoon water
fresh white breadcrumbs	fresh soft white bread crumbs
deep fat for frying	deep fat for frying
150 ml/¼ pint Chicken stock (page 55)	⅔ cup Chicken stock (page 55)
150 ml/¼ pint cream	⅔ cup cream
25 g/1 oz butter	2 tablespoons butter
Corn fritters (page 123) to serve	Corn fritters (page 123) to serve
garnish:	*garnish:*
4 crisp bacon rolls or rashers	4 crisp bacon rolls or slices
4 small bananas	4 small bananas
lemon wedges	lemon wedges

Joint and skin the chicken (page 65). Divide the legs into two joints and separate the wings from the breasts. Flour the joints, patting off any excess. Beat the egg and water together and brush over each joint. Place it on a bed of crumbs, cover with more crumbs and press well in. Shake off any surplus and set aside for the coating to harden for 1 hour or longer.

Heat about 3 cm/1½ inches of fat in a large, thick frying pan to 190°C/380°F. Give each joint a final shake and fry until golden underneath, pressing the wings flat if they curl out of the fat. Turn the joints and fry on the other side until golden. Lower the heat slightly and continue frying for about 10 minutes each side, a total of 35–40 minutes.

Cover during cooking with a ventilated lid or, if the lid has no vent, tilt it so the steam can escape. Drain the cooked chicken on soft paper and keep warm.

Fry the corn fritters in the hot fat, drain and keep warm. Carefully pour off the fat, leaving the juices in the pan. Stir in a tablespoon of seasoned flour and fry, stirring for a few minutes. Blend in the stock and cream, simmer gently for 3 minutes and pour into a warm sauce boat. Meanwhile, in another pan, fry the bacon (or grill bacon rolls) until crisp, remove and add the butter. Peel and halve the bananas lengthwise and fry briskly.

Arrange the chicken on a warm serving dish and garnish with the bacon, bananas and lemon. Serve with the corn fritters and sauce. *Serves 4*

Chicken in a basket

This is the simplest way to fry chicken and is an ideal dish to serve hot at a fork-and-finger party in the garden or cold at a picnic.

For large parties it is more economical to buy trays of drumsticks and/or chicken breasts instead of jointing whole chickens. The drumsticks are most convenient to hold in the fingers.

METRIC/IMPERIAL	AMERICAN
6 chicken drumsticks	6 chicken drumsticks
seasoned flour for coating	seasoned flour for coating
1 egg	1 egg
4 teaspoons Dijon mustard	4 teaspoons Dijon mustard
175 g/6 oz fresh breadcrumbs	3 cups fresh soft bread crumbs
4 tablespoons grated cheese	$\frac{1}{3}$ cup grated cheese
deep fat for frying	deep fat for frying
watercress or parsley to garnish	watercress or parsley to garnish

Wipe and dry the chicken and thaw out thoroughly if frozen. Toss in seasoned flour, patting off any surplus. Beat the egg and gradually blend into the mustard.

Mix together the breadcrumbs and grated cheese and make a bed of this on a piece of greaseproof paper. Take the joints, one at a time, and brush carefully all over with egg and mustard. Then place on the bed of crumbs and cheese and, by tipping the paper, roll the joint over in the crumbs until completely coated. Press the crumbs in firmly. Shake off any surplus and leave the coating to harden before deep frying.

After frying, drain on soft paper. Cover the protruding ends of the bones with cutlet frills, if liked. Arrange in a basket lined with a napkin and garnish with watercress or parsley sprigs. *Serves 4–6*

Serving suggestions: Serve hot with tomato or Barbecue sauce (page 96). Accompany with jacket potatoes stuffed with cottage cheese and chopped chives or hot potato and crispy bacon salad, or French garlic bread (page 123). Serve cold with Tartare or Gribiche sauce (page 100). Accompany with salads (which can be dressed in advance and easily eaten with a fork), tomato, cucumber, green peppers and chopped spring onions with French dressing; chicory, apple, celery and beetroot with sour cream dressing and new potato salad.

Bird in pies and pastries

Crispy golden pastry, as well as contributing to variety in menus, is a marvellous stretcher of poultry.

As little as 100 g/4 oz cooked chicken meat will make a tasty filling for Kromeskies or 175 g/6 oz for Alsatian chicken and cheese tart (pages 111 and 36).

Welsh leek and chicken pie

This pie has a particularly tasty filling of chicken mixed with a creamy leek and bacon sauce. A small boiling fowl will make a large family-sized pie, and the same recipe with reduced quantities, using surplus cooked chicken, can be used as a flavoursome filling for Vols-au-vent (page 24), Piroshki (page 35) and Kromeskies (page 111).

METRIC/IMPERIAL	AMERICAN
1 small boiling chicken, cooked (page 57)	1 small stewing chicken, cooked (page 57)
225 g/8 oz leeks	$\frac{1}{2}$ lb leeks
100 g/4 oz bacon rashers	$\frac{1}{4}$ lb bacon slices
25 g/1 oz butter	2 tablespoons butter
1$\frac{1}{2}$ tablespoons flour	2 tablespoons flour
450 ml/$\frac{3}{4}$ pint chicken stock	2 cups chicken stock
150 ml/$\frac{1}{4}$ pint single cream	$\frac{2}{3}$ cup light cream
salt and freshly ground black pepper	salt and freshly ground black pepper
lemon juice to taste	lemon juice to taste
1 (368-g/13-oz) packet frozen puff pastry, thawed	1 (13-oz) package frozen puff pastry, thawed
beaten egg to glaze	beaten egg to glaze

Skin the chicken, remove the flesh from the bones and cut into chunks.

Clean the leeks, remove most of the green and cut into 1-cm/$\frac{1}{2}$-inch slices. Remove the rind and gristle from the bacon and chop across into strips; heat slowly in a thick saucepan until the fat runs and the bacon begins to crisp. Add the butter and, when melted, the leeks. Cover and cook gently, without colouring, until softened. Stir frequently. Remove the pan from the heat and blend in the flour and then two-thirds of the chicken stock. Simmer and cook for 5 minutes, stirring well. Blend the remaining stock into the cream. Remove the leek sauce from the heat and stir in the cream mixture. Season well and sharpen with lemon juice. Mix in the chicken pieces.

Roll out the pastry; cover, decorate and glaze the pie. Bake in a hot oven (230°C, 450°F, Gas Mark 8) for 10–15 minutes until the pastry is well risen. Lower the heat to moderately hot (200°C, 400°F, Gas Mark 6) and continue cooking for a further 20 minutes or until crisp and golden. *Serves 6*

To decorate a pie crust

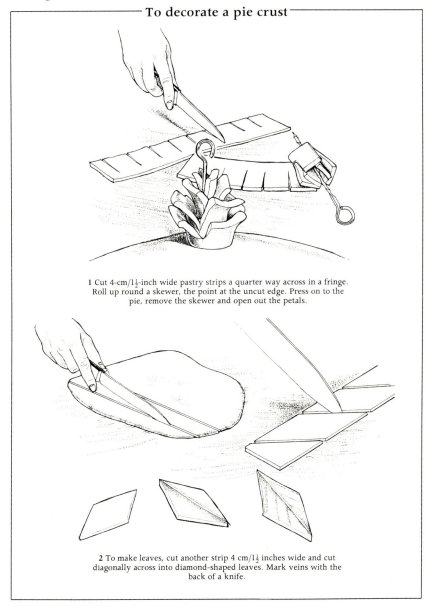

1 Cut 4-cm/1½-inch wide pastry strips a quarter way across in a fringe. Roll up round a skewer, the point at the uncut edge. Press on to the pie, remove the skewer and open out the petals.

2 To make leaves, cut another strip 4 cm/1½ inches wide and cut diagonally across into diamond-shaped leaves. Mark veins with the back of a knife.

Chicken en croûte

The top chef's style for this dish is a whole bird, boned and filled with a rich stuffing, roasted French style and then wrapped in puff pastry, elaborately decorated and baked. The following recipe, using chicken joints, is an easy but delicious version for the home cook to make.

METRIC/IMPERIAL	AMERICAN
4 chicken joints from a young bird	4 chicken pieces from a young bird
1 (368-g/13-oz) packet frozen puff pastry, thawed	1 (13-oz) package frozen puff pastry, thawed
5 tablespoons cranberry and orange relish or a similar chutney	6 tablespoons cranberry and orange relish or a similar chutney
1 egg	1 egg
1 tablespoon water	1 tablespoon water

The joints can be breasts, thighs or drumsticks, as available. If the croûtes are to be eaten hot, remove the bones neatly and press the flesh back together. If they are to be eaten cold at a picnic, choose chicken drumsticks and leave the end of the bone protruding from the pastry. When cooked, it can be covered with a frill and held in the fingers.

Roll the pastry out very thinly. Space the joints out on the pastry and cut round. Lift up each joint, one at a time, spread with relish on both sides and place it back on the pastry. Cut a top for each joint.

Beat the egg and water together and brush round the edge. Place the pastry top on the joint and press the edges firmly together. Knock up with the back of a knife. Brush all over with beaten egg. Decorate with little leaves, cut from the pastry trimmings and glaze. Make two or three slits for the steam to escape.

Bake in a hot oven (220°C, 425°F, Gas Mark 7) for 15 minutes until well risen and golden. Reduce the heat to moderately hot (190°C, 375°F, Gas Mark 5) and continue baking for 15–20 minutes, until the joints are thoroughly cooked. Serve hot or cold with tossed salad. *Serves 4*

Variation: For a richer dish, mix 50 g/2 oz (U.S. $\frac{1}{2}$ cup) finely chopped mushrooms with 50 g/2 oz (U.S. $\frac{1}{4}$ cup) liver pâté and use instead of chutney.

Chicken and ham pie à la Russe

(Illustrated on page 34)

This attractive dish is delightfully quick to make if frozen pastry is used. The ingredients for the filling can be varied to use up cooked chicken meat and ham as available. The cheese melts during baking and makes the filling succulent as well as savoury. If liked replace the cheese with extra mushrooms.

METRIC/IMPERIAL	AMERICAN
100–150 g/4–5 oz cooked chicken, chopped	$\frac{1}{2}$–$\frac{1}{3}$ cup chopped cooked chicken
50 g/2 oz cooked ham, diced	$\frac{1}{4}$ cup diced cooked ham
150 g/5 oz Cheddar cheese, diced	1$\frac{1}{4}$ cups diced Cheddar cheese
50 g/2 oz mushrooms, chopped	$\frac{1}{2}$ cup chopped mushrooms
1 tablespoon chopped parsley	1 tablespoon chopped parsley
salt and freshly ground black pepper	salt and freshly ground black pepper
1 egg	1 egg
225 g/8 oz frozen puff pastry, thawed	$\frac{1}{2}$ lb frozen puff pastry, thawed
beaten egg to glaze	beaten egg to glaze

Mix together the chicken, ham, cheese, mushrooms and parsley. Season to taste. Stir 1 beaten egg into the mixture. Roll the pastry thinly into a rectangle 39 × 26 cm/15 × 10 inches. Cut out a 26-cm/10-inch square (see below). Place on a baking tray. Pile the filling in the centre. Fold the corners of the square to the centre and seal with beaten egg. Brush all over the pie evenly with egg. Use any remaining pastry to make decorations and a tassel (page 25), glaze with egg and arrange on the pie. Open the outer corners of the envelope slightly to allow steam to escape during cooking.

Bake in a hot oven (220°C, 425°F, Gas Mark 7) for 25 minutes until well risen and golden brown. Serve hot with tomato quarters and fresh watercress. *Serves 4–6*

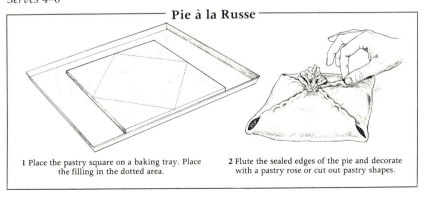

Pie à la Russe

1 Place the pastry square on a baking tray. Place the filling in the dotted area.

2 Flute the sealed edges of the pie and decorate with a pastry rose or cut out pastry shapes.

Country chicken and mushroom pie

METRIC/IMPERIAL	AMERICAN
1 small boiling chicken	1 small stewing chicken
1 medium onion, chopped	1 medium onion, chopped
1 stick celery, chopped	1 stalk celery, chopped
1–2 carrots, sliced	1–2 carrots, sliced
1 bay leaf	1 bay leaf
1 sprig parsley	1 sprig parsley
1 sprig thyme or rosemary	1 sprig thyme or rosemary
salt and freshly ground	salt and freshly ground
black pepper	black pepper
50 g/2 oz belly of pork,	2 oz salt pork,
pickled or smoked	pickled or smoked
1 (370-g/13-oz) packet frozen	1 (13-oz) package frozen
puff pastry, thawed	puff pastry, thawed
75 g/3 oz mushrooms, sliced	1 cup sliced mushrooms
beaten egg to glaze	beaten egg to glaze
sauce:	*sauce:*
50 g/2 oz butter or	$\frac{1}{4}$ cup butter or
margarine	margarine
40 g/1$\frac{1}{2}$ oz flour	6 tablespoons flour
150 ml/$\frac{1}{4}$ pint milk	$\frac{2}{3}$ cup milk
1 teaspoon lemon juice	1 teaspoon lemon juice
2 tablespoons chopped parsley	3 tablespoons chopped parsley

Boil the bird in enough water to cover with the onion, celery, carrot, bay leaf, parsley and thyme or rosemary and seasoning. This will take about 1$\frac{1}{2}$ hours. When the bird is cooked, lift it from the pan, remove the flesh and cut it into neat pieces. Strain the stock and skim off the fat.

Dice the belly of pork and mix with the chicken meat. Then make the sauce. Melt the butter, stir in the flour and remove the pan from the heat. Gradually add the milk, stirring continuously. Still stirring, bring to simmering point then stir in 150 ml/$\frac{1}{4}$ pint (U. S. $\frac{2}{3}$ cup) of the reserved stock. Season with lemon juice, salt and pepper and stir in the parsley. Mix in the chicken and turn into a deep oval pie dish with a pie funnel in the centre. Cover with the sliced mushrooms. Allow to become quite cold.

Roll out the pastry to 5 mm/$\frac{1}{4}$ inch thick, damp the rim of the dish and cover with a strip of pastry cut from the outside of the whole. Brush the rim with water and cover with the remaining pastry. Press the edges together and trim off the surplus. Knock up and flute the edges. Cut two slits for the steam to escape and make a hole into the pie funnel with a skewer. Brush the top with beaten egg and decorate with any pastry trimmings made into leaves. Glaze the decorations and bake the pie in a hot oven (230°C, 450°F, Gas Mark 8) for 20 minutes. Reduce to moderately hot (190°C, 375°F, Gas Mark 5) for a further 20 minutes or until the pastry is completely cooked. *Serves 4*

Hot vols-au-vent

These are always popular and can be made quite tiny for cocktail savouries or full size for a main course.

Make or buy vol-au-vent cases. Heat the cases and, when ready to serve, fill with hot Cheesy chicken à la King (page 115) or chopped cooked chicken in Blanquette or Cheese béchamel sauce (pages 93 and 99). If they are filled before heating, the pastry cases will not be so crisp.

Cold vols-au-vent

Make or buy extra light puff pastry cases if they are to be eaten cold, as they will not be crisped by reheating. Fill them with chopped chicken and cucumber mixed with Tuna mayonnaise (page 100), or combined with diced cooked tongue or lean ham mixed with Gribiche sauce (page 100).

To make vol-au-vent cases

To make vol-au-vent cases, cut out circles of pastry with a plain cutter. Cut out the centres of half the pastry circles to make rings. Brush one side of the rings with water and press firmly on to the base.

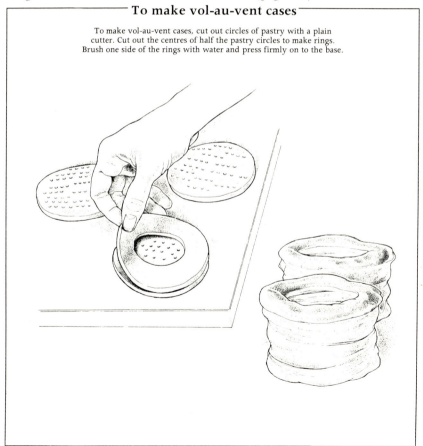

Raised chicken pie

This cold pie can also be made with any combination of game and poultry. The knuckle of veal provides extra meat as well as providing jelly in the stock.

METRIC/IMPERIAL	AMERICAN
40 g/1½ oz butter	3 tablespoons butter
1 chicken	1 chicken
225 g/8 oz pickled belly pork, cut in chunks	½ lb salt pork, cut in chunks
1 knuckle veal, cut in three	1 veal shank, cut in three
1 onion, sliced	1 onion, sliced
1–2 sticks celery, chopped	1–2 stalks celery, chopped
2–3 carrots, scraped	2–3 carrots, cleaned
1 bouquet garni	1 bouquet garni
6 tablespoons red wine	½ cup red wine
salt and freshly ground black pepper	salt and freshly ground black pepper
1 quantity Hot water crust pastry (page 32)	1 quantity Hot water crust pastry (page 32)
beaten egg to glaze	beaten egg to glaze

Heat the butter in a flameproof casserole and brown the bird all over or roast in a hot oven (220°C, 425°F, Gas Mark 7) for 15 minutes. Lift out of the casserole, remove the breasts and set aside. Mix the pork, veal and onion together in the hot butter and fry gently until just coloured. Break up and add the carcass and cleaned giblets, the celery, carrots, herbs and wine. Cover with cold water, season well and bring to the boil. Cover and simmer gently for 2 hours. Remove the thighs when they are tender. Strain the stock and leave to cool into a jelly. Skim off the fat. Remove the flesh from the carcass and veal knuckle and mince or chop finely. Discard the bones, vegetables and herbs but retain the pork chunks. Cut the breast and thighs into neat pieces. Line the pie mould or 15-cm/6-inch cake tin with a loose base, with hot water crust pastry. Season the minced meat to taste and spread over the base of the pie. Fill up with well-mixed chicken and pork meat and moisten with a very little stock.

Cover, decorate (page 25) and glaze with beaten egg, making slits in the top. Bake in a moderately hot oven (200°C, 400°F, Gas Mark 6) for 30 minutes or until the pie is golden brown and set. Open the mould and remove the sides. If using a cake tin, stand it on an inverted jam jar and carefully push down the sides of the tin, leaving the mould on the base. Brush the sides of the pie with beaten egg, cover the top with greaseproof paper, return to the oven and bake for a further 20–30 minutes, until the sides are brown.

Meanwhile check that the stock has set into jelly; if not, boil it until reduced, correct the seasoning and cool.

Remove the pie from the oven and, using a little funnel, carefully pour the cool liquid jelly through the slits into the pie, or through the hole under the pastry rose or tassel, giving it time to trickle between the meat chunks and fill the crevices.

Serve the pie, when cold, with cranberry relish or apricot chutney. Accompany with potato and other dressed salads in season. *Serves 4–6*

Raised pie

1 Shape the hot water crust into a fat sausage. Cut off one-third and keep warm in a polythene bag.

2 Roll out the remaining dough on a floured board into an oval about 1 cm/½ inch thick

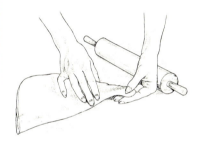

3 Flour the surface lightly and evenly and fold the oval in half to make a semi-circle. With a floured rolling pin, roll lightly away from you until the dough is 1 cm/½ inch thick. Do not press heavily or the dough will stick together.

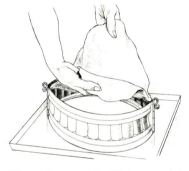

4 Now gently open out the folded pastry and slip it into the greased pie mould, placed on a baking tray. Press the dough evenly over the base, well into the corners and up the sides of the mould. Put the filling in.

5 Roll out the remaining dough to 5 mm/¼ inch thick to make a lid. Brush the rim of the dough lining the mould with water, place the lid in position and press the edges firmly together. Trim the edges with scissors and mark evenly with the back of a knife to make a neat edge.

6 Crimp the edge with your fingers and use the dough trimmings to decorate the top.

Hot water crust pastry

METRIC/IMPERIAL
275 g/10 oz plain flour
¼ teaspoon salt
75 g/3 oz lard or cooking fat
150 ml/¼ pint water

AMERICAN
2½ cups all-purpose flour
¼ teaspoon salt
6 tablespoons lard or shortening
⅔ cup water

Sift the flour and salt into a warm mixing bowl. Put the fat and water into a small saucepan over a low heat. When the fat has dissolved, bring the liquid to the boil. Pour immediately into the flour, stirring with a wooden spoon and beat into a ball. Knead the pastry on a floured board until it forms a smooth ball. Put this in a polythene bag, wrap in a warm tea towel and keep warm until required.

Shortcrust pastry

METRIC/IMPERIAL
225 g/8 oz plain flour
pinch of salt
125 g/4 oz butter, margarine
or lard

AMERICAN
2 cups all-purpose flour
dash of salt
½ cup butter, margarine
or lard

Sift the flour and salt into a mixing bowl. Cut up the fat and, with the tips of the fingers, rub it into the flour until the mixture resembles breadcrumbs. Hold the hands well above the bowl to aerate the mixture and keep it cool. Shake the bowl to bring the larger crumbs to the surface for rubbing in. Do not over-rub or the fat will become oily and the pastry heavy. Add cold water, a tablespoon at a time, and stir it in with a palette knife until the mixture binds into a soft, but not sticky dough. Too much water makes the pastry heavy, too little will make it crumbly. Gather it together with one hand, it should leave the sides of the bowl clean. Turn on to a floured board and knead lightly until the cracks disappear. Leave in a cool place until required.

Roast farmhouse chicken (see page 14)

Chicken piroshki

These little Polish pasties are ideal for a fireside supper or hot buffet dish. They can be made with shortcrust or flaky pastry and any available mixture of chicken, game, pork or ham.

METRIC/IMPERIAL	AMERICAN
2 large shallots, sliced	2 large shallots, sliced
50 g/2 oz mushrooms, chopped	$\frac{1}{2}$ cup chopped mushrooms
50 g/2 oz belly pork or ham, diced	$\frac{1}{3}$ cup diced salt pork or cooked ham
25 g/1 oz butter	2 tablespoons butter
100 g/4 oz cooked chicken, chopped	$\frac{1}{2}$ cup chopped cooked chicken
1 teaspoon dried savory or rosemary	1 teaspoon dried savory or rosemary
1 tablespoon chopped parsley	1 tablespoon chopped parsley
salt and freshly ground black pepper	salt and freshly ground black pepper
3–4 tablespoons soured cream	4–5 tablespoons dairy sour cream
225 g/8 oz Shortcrust (page 32) or flaky pastry	$\frac{1}{2}$ lb Shortcrust (page 32) or flaky pastry
beaten egg to glaze	beaten egg to glaze

Fry the finely sliced shallots, mushrooms and pork slowly in the butter until slightly crisp. Mix in the chicken or game and herbs and cook gently until well buttered. Season well, stir in the soured cream (or double cream sharpened with lemon juice) and leave to cool.

Roll out the pastry thinly. Cut out eight circles and line Yorkshire pudding or deep patty tins. Spoon in the filling. Cut eight smaller circles from the remaining pastry. Damp the pastry edges and press the lids in place, pinching the edges firmly together. Crimp with a fork. Brush the tops with beaten egg and cut little slits in the centre for the steam to escape. Bake in a hot oven (220°C, 425°F, Gas Mark 7) until crisp and golden. *Makes 8*

Chicken and ham pie à la Russe (see page 27)

Alsatian chicken and cheese tart

This tart served hot makes an appetising main course for lunch or supper. It is good picnic fare when served cold.

METRIC/IMPERIAL	AMERICAN
175 g/6 oz Shortcrust pastry (page 32)	1½ cups Shortcrust pastry (page 32)
25 g/1 oz butter	2 tablespoons butter
2 rashers streaky bacon, chopped	2 bacon slices, chopped
1 small onion, chopped	1 small onion, chopped
250 ml/8 fl oz cream	1 cup cream
50 g/2 oz cheese, grated	½ cup grated cheese
175 g/6 oz cooked chicken	6 oz cooked chicken
1 egg	1 egg
paprika	paprika pepper
salt and freshly ground black pepper	salt and freshly ground black pepper

Roll out the pastry thinly. Damp the lip of a 20-cm/8-inch shallow pie plate and press on 1-cm/½-inch wide strips of pastry. Brush with water. Roll the remaining pastry round the rolling pin and unroll across the pie plate. Ease the pastry lining into the dish and press firmly round the edge to prevent shrinkage in the oven. Trim neatly and knock up the edges with the back of the knife. Using a small fluted cutter, cut pastry circles out of the trimmings. Dampen the pastry on the lip of the dish and press on the circles, marking the centre of each one with a skewer. Prick over the base of the pie.

Heat the butter in a small pan and fry the bacon and onion slowly until just colouring. Add the cream and heat until nearly boiling. Remove from the heat and stir in the cheese. When melted add the chicken. Stir in the beaten egg and season well with paprika, salt and pepper.

Pour the mixture into the pie and bake in a moderately hot oven (190°C, 375°F, Gas Mark 5) for 20 minutes or until set and nicely coloured.

Serve hot or cold with asparagus spears or a mixed salad tossed in French dressing. *Serves 4–6*

Alsatian chicken and cheese tart

1 Press a 1-cm/½-inch wide strip of pastry round the lip of the pie plate.

2 Ease the pastry lining into the dish and press firmly round the edges.

3 Knock up the edge with the back of a knife.

4 Press the pastry decorations round the dampened ring.

Chicken and apple pasties

This is a tasty way of using up the remains of cooked chicken. The quantity can be stretched with cooked ham as convenient. The pasties can be served hot for lunch, high tea or supper or cold for a packed lunch.

METRIC/IMPERIAL	AMERICAN
225 g/8 oz cooked chicken meat or half chicken and half cooked ham	1 cup chopped cooked chicken meat or half chicken and half cooked ham
1 medium onion, finely chopped	1 medium onion, finely chopped
1 large or 2 small Bramley apples, peeled, cored and chopped	1 large or 2 small baking apples, peeled, cored and chopped
1 teaspoon coriander seed, crushed	1 teaspoon coriander seed, crushed
2–3 tablespoons chicken stock	3–4 tablespoons chicken stock
salt and freshly ground black pepper	salt and freshly ground black pepper
225 g/8 oz Shortcrust pastry (page 32)	2 cups Shortcrust pastry (page 32)
beaten egg to glaze	beaten egg to glaze

Mix together the meat, onion, apple and coriander. Add enough stock to moisten the mixture. Season to taste.

Roll out the pastry on a lightly floured surface and cut out four 13-cm/5-inch rounds, using a small plate as a guide. Divide the filling into four and put a quarter in the centre of each pastry round. Brush the pastry edges with water and draw the two sides together over the filling. Press together to make Cornish pasty shapes. Crimp the edges or mark with a fork. Cut three slits on either side of the pasties to let the steam escape.

Place the pasties on a baking tray and glaze with beaten egg. If there are any trimmings, roll them out and cut out decorations. Place them on the pasties and glaze.

Bake in a hot oven (220°C, 425°F, Gas Mark 7) for 20 minutes or until risen and golden. *Serves 4*

Cold bird

Poultry can be made into a wide variety of attractive cold dishes. It can be boiled, or oven- or spit-roasted and, when cold, served with a rich sauce to counterbalance any dryness. Smaller quantities can be chopped to make a salad or a mousse.

Cold chicken with tuna sauce

This Italian summer dish is much easier and quicker to prepare than the classic chaudfroid of chicken. It is also an appetising way to use up surplus joints of a chicken which has been spit- or oven-roasted.

METRIC/IMPERIAL	AMERICAN
1 boiling or roasting chicken	1 stewing or roaster chicken
300 ml/$\frac{1}{2}$ pint Tuna mayonnaise (page 100)	1$\frac{1}{4}$ cups Tuna mayonnaise (page 100)
strained stock	strained stock
$\frac{1}{2}$ cucumber or 1 (78-g/ 2$\frac{3}{4}$-oz) can pimientos	$\frac{1}{2}$ cucumber or 1 (2$\frac{3}{4}$-oz) can pimientos
curly endive or lettuce and radishes	curly endive or lettuce and radishes

Boil the bird (page 57) or roast (page 14) and skin while still warm. When cold, remove the legs and separate the drumsticks and thigh joints. Carefully carve off the breast in two complete fillets and remove the wings, leaving the *suprêmes* (breasts). If they are large, slice each of these slantwise in half. Make a double quantity of the recipe for tuna mayonnaise and, if necessary, thin it with a little strained stock. The sauce should be the consistency to coat the back of a wooden spoon evenly and fairly thickly. Place the joints on a plate, coat carefully with the sauce, and decorate with strips of cucumber or pimiento. Chill the joints until set and then lift carefully on to a serving dish or individual plates. Garnish with curly endive or lettuce leaves and prepared radishes.

Serve with a salad of sliced new potatoes tossed in French dressing and garnished with chives or chopped spring onions. *Serves 6*

Chicken salamagundy

Salamagundy was considered a 'fine middle dish' for a fashionable table in 18th-century England and the modern version makes a splendid centre piece for a buffet table to which the guests can help themselves.

METRIC/IMPERIAL	AMERICAN
1 (1·5–2-kg/3½–4-lb) chicken, cooked	1 (3½–4-lb) chicken, cooked
1 bunch spring onions	1 bunch scallions
150 ml/¼ pint Thick mayonnaise (page 100)	⅔ cup Thick mayonnaise (page 100)
1 tablespoon chopped parsley	1 tablespoon chopped parsley
150 ml/¼ pint double cream	⅔ cup heavy cream
1 lemon	1 lemon
salt and freshly ground black pepper	salt and freshly ground black pepper
2 hard-boiled eggs	2 hard-cooked eggs
½ cucumber, sliced	½ cucumber, sliced
1 bunch watercress	1 bunch watercress
1 lettuce	1 head lettuce
50 g/2 oz mushrooms	½ cup mushrooms
1 bunch radishes	1 bunch radishes
150 ml/¼ pint French dressing	⅔ cup French dressing

Skin the chicken. Slice the chicken breast into fingers and set aside. Remove the flesh from the legs and the rest of the carcass and chop into small pieces. Clean the spring onions leaving 5–7·5 cm/2–3 inches of green. Chop them finely and add to the mayonnaise, which must be very thick. Stir in the parsley. Whip the cream until thick and fold in the mayonnaise.

Peel and chop the lemon, removing the pith and skin and mix it with the chopped chicken. Stir in sufficient cream and mayonnaise mixture to bind. Season to taste with salt and pepper.

Separate the yolks and whites of the eggs. Sieve the yolks to make mimosa and chop the whites with a stainless steel knife. Pile the chicken mayonnaise mixture into the centre of a large round dish and decorate the top of the mound with circles of mimosa egg, chopped white and chopped parsley.

Surround with circles of sliced cucumber, washed watercress sprigs and arrange mushroom slices and prepared lettuce leaves round the outside of the dish. Arrange the chicken fingers on the watercress. Wash and trim the radishes and put one between each chicken finger. Sprinkle the chicken with mimosa egg. Just before serving, sprinkle the green salad with French dressing. *Serves 6–8*

Chaudfroid of chicken

METRIC/IMPERIAL	AMERICAN
1 cooked chicken	1 cooked chicken
450 ml/¾ pint Chaudfroid sauce	2 cups Chaudfroid sauce
(below)	(below)
watercress and cucumber	watercress and cucumber
900 ml/1½ pints Chicken aspic	3¾ cups Chicken aspic
jelly (page 56)	jelly (page 56)
salad vegetables to garnish	salad vegetables to garnish

Skin and carve the cold bird as in the preceding recipe, but remove the bones from the joints and reshape. Or, leave the bird whole. Cool the chaudfroid sauce to coating consistency, spoon evenly over the bird and leave to set.

Pull the leaves off the watercress stalks, and cut the unpeeled cucumber in thin slices and quarter. Arrange in a simple bold design of watercress sprigs and overlapping cucumber triangles on the chopping board, then transfer this on to the bird, dipping each item in the cool liquid aspic jelly before setting in position. Leave until firmly set on the sauce, then coat all over with the jelly, which is tacky but sufficiently liquid to spoon evenly over the bird. Leave to set and coat a second time if necessary.

When firmly set, arrange the bird on a serving dish and surround with the remaining chopped aspic jelly. Garnish with salad vegetables. *Serves 4–6*

Chaudfroid sauce

for coating cold bird and galantine

Make a Velouté sauce (page 95), using strained chicken stock which has set into a firm jelly and then been melted down. Cool the sauce in a bowl of cold water, stirring frequently until it is the right coating consistency for the chaudfroid dish.

Chicken and ham mousse

This is a super way to transform a small quantity of surplus cooked chicken into an elegant dish, which can be served either as a starter or a main course. If larger quantities are needed, perhaps for a summer buffet party, a boiling fowl, cooked according to the recipe on page 57, would be the most economical buy.

METRIC/IMPERIAL	AMERICAN
150 ml/$\frac{3}{4}$ pint Chicken aspic jelly (page 56)	$\frac{2}{3}$ cup Chicken aspic jelly (page 56)
15 g/$\frac{1}{2}$ oz butter	1 tablespoon butter
15 g/$\frac{1}{2}$ oz flour	2 tablespoons flour
150 ml/$\frac{1}{4}$ pint Chicken stock (page 55)	$\frac{2}{3}$ cup Chicken stock (page 55)
1 egg, separated	1 egg, separated
3 tablespoons cream	$\frac{1}{4}$ cup cream
15 g/$\frac{1}{2}$ oz powdered gelatine	2 envelopes gelatin
3 tablespoons boiling water	$\frac{1}{4}$ cup boiling water
175 g/6 oz cooked chicken, minced	$\frac{3}{4}$ cup ground cooked chicken
50 g/2 oz lean ham, minced	$\frac{1}{4}$ cup ground cooked lean ham
1 teaspoon tomato ketchup	1 teaspoon tomato ketchup
few drops of Worcestershire sauce	few drops of Worcestershire sauce
lemon juice to taste	lemon juice to taste
salt and freshly ground black pepper	salt and freshly ground black pepper
tomato, cucumber and watercress to garnish	tomato, cucumber and watercress to garnish

Melt the chicken jelly and set aside to cool or use aspic jelly crystals according to the instructions on the packet.

Make a thick white sauce (see Panada, page 95) with the butter, flour and chicken stock. Beat the egg yolk and cream together and stir into the sauce. Dissolve the gelatine thoroughly in the boiling water and then stir into the sauce. Add the chicken and ham. Flavour to taste with ketchup, Worcestershire sauce and lemon juice and season well, remembering that the flavour of a chilled dish tends to be blander than that of a hot one.

Whisk the egg white until stiff, but not brittle, and fold the mixture carefully into it. Pour into a soufflé dish or individual ramekins, smooth the top and chill well.

When set, decorate with the garnishing vegetables in an attractive pattern: dip each piece of vegetable into the cool liquid jelly and arrange on top of the mousse. Chill until the pattern is firm, then carefully spoon over another layer of jelly and allow to set. This looks attractive and prevents the garnish from wilting. *Serves 4 as a main course, 6 as a starter*

Chicken and ham mousse

1 Lay the pattern out on a board.

2 Transfer the garnish to the mousse, dipping each piece of vegetable in cool liquid jelly. Leave to set.

3 Spoon over a second layer of jelly and allow to set.

Cold galantine of chicken

This is an excellent dish for a cold buffet or luncheon party, as the boned and stuffed bird presents no carving problems and looks very attractive when decorated and glazed with chaudfroid sauce or aspic jelly. Boning the chicken and cooling the sauce and jelly to the right consistency can be tricky, but very rewarding for the fairly experienced and adventurous cook.

METRIC/IMPERIAL	AMERICAN
1 boiling chicken	1 stewing chicken
1 knuckle veal	1 veal shank
vegetables, herbs and seasoning	vegetables, herbs and seasoning
for Chicken stock (page 55)	for Chicken stock (page 55)
Farce for galantine (page 122)	Farce for galantine (page 122)
100 g/4 oz cooked tongue, diced	¾ cup diced cooked tongue
300 ml/½ pint Chicken aspic	1¼ cups Chicken aspic
jelly (page 56)	jelly (page 56)
450 ml/¾ pint Chaudfroid sauce	2 cups Chaudfroid sauce
(page 41)	(page 41)
watercress, tarragon, curly endive	watercress, tarragon, curly endive
or salad to garnish	or salad to garnish

Bone the bird (see opposite) and set aside. Prepare the carcass, bones and giblets and put into a large pan with the knuckle of veal, chopped into three or four pieces, and the other ingredients for the chicken stock (page 55). Add 2·25 litres/4 pints (U. S. 10 cups) cold water. Bring to the boil, skim and simmer until required.

Meanwhile, lay the boned fowl out on a board. Cover with the galantine farce and sprinkle with the diced tongue. Fold over the sides of the bird and mould it as far as possible to its original shape. Sew up the openings with coarse thread or secure with small poultry skewers laced with fine string. Wrap in a muslin cloth and tie the ends so the bird can be easily lifted in and out of the pan.

Put it into the pan, making sure the stock covers it completely. Simmer very gently for 2–3 hours according to size and age. When tender, lift carefully from the pan. Boil up the stock, then strain, cool, remove the fat and use to make the aspic jelly and chaudfroid sauce. Leave the chicken to cool and set overnight. If liked, it may be pressed between two plates with a weight on the top one.

Next day remove the string and skewers. Coat evenly with cool chaudfroid sauce. Decorate with watercress or tarragon leaves, dipping each one in cool aspic jelly before putting in position. Leave to set then coat the whole bird with aspic jelly, which should be tacky but sufficiently liquid to flow evenly. Leave again to set firmly. Using a hot knife, chop up the remaining jelly when set. Place the galantine on a serving dish and garnish with chopped jelly, watercress or curly endive, cucumber slices and tomato wedges or radishes.

If preferred, the chaudfroid sauce may be omitted and the galantine glazed with aspic jelly only, coating twice. *Serves 6–8*

Cold galatine of chicken

1 Turn the chicken breast downwards and slit the skin down the centre back of the bird.

2 Work the skin and flesh from the carcass until the thigh joint is reached. Insert the knife between the ball and socket of the joint, sever the sinew and remove the thigh bone.

3 Hold the end of the joint between the fingers and work the meat off the drumstick and remove the bone completely.

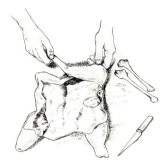

4 Sever the wing joint from the body and work the flesh off the breastbone. Repeat on the other wing. Carefully ease the skin off the breastbone without cutting and remove the breastbone.

5 Flatten the bird on a board and cover with the galantine farce. Sprinkle with chopped tongue.

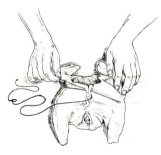

6 Fold the sides of the bird over and mould as far as possible to the original shape. Sew up with a trussing needle and coarse thread. Turn over and truss.

Chicken and fruit curry

This is a versatile dish in which the fresh fruits can be varied according to the season. In winter, plumped dried apricots, peaches and prunes can be used and canned pineapple and mangoes if fresh are not available. The curry sauce should be spicy but mild, as a fiery sauce will kill the delicate flavours of the fruit. It also makes the dish acceptable as a starter – which must never be so pungent that the next course cannot be tasted.

METRIC/IMPERIAL	AMERICAN
1 tablespoon desiccated coconut	1 tablespoon shredded coconut
150 ml/¼ pint boiling water	⅔ cup boiling water
2 small onions, thinly sliced	2 small onions, thinly sliced
50 g/2 oz butter	¼ cup butter
2 tablespoons flour	3 tablespoons flour
2 teaspoons curry powder	2 teaspoons curry powder
1 teaspoon curry paste	1 teaspoon curry paste
1 teaspoon crushed coriander seeds	1 teaspoon crushed coriander seeds
2 knobs stem ginger, chopped	2 knobs stem ginger, chopped
600 ml/1 pint Chicken stock (page 55)	2½ cups Chicken stock (page 55)
450 g/1 lb prepared fruit (see method)	1 lb prepared fruit (see method)
350 g/12 oz cooked chicken meat	¾ lb cooked chicken meat
5 tablespoons double cream	6 tablespoons heavy cream
1–2 tablespoons lemon juice	1–3 tablespoons lemon juice
salt to taste	salt to taste

Soak the coconut in the boiling water until required.

Fry the onions lightly in the butter. Remove from the heat and stir in the flour, curry powder and paste, coriander and ginger. Return to the heat and continue cooking gently for 5 minutes. Blend in the strained coconut liquid and the stock and simmer for 30 minutes.

Prepare the fruit: peel, core or stone, cut into neat pieces and add to the pan. Cut the chicken into pieces and mix into the curry sauce, and then add the cream. Sharpen to taste with lemon juice and season with salt. Serve hot or ice cold.

For a first course put the chilled curry into small individual glass bowls. Stand each one in a large bowl or soup dish, surround with crushed ice and garnish with a few fresh mint leaves. Hand crisply fried poppadums separately.

For a main dish, serve with fluffy boiled rice, chappatis, naan or poppadums.
Serves 4 as a main course, 6 as a starter

Chicken and ham salad

METRIC/IMPERIAL
350–450 g/12 oz–1 lb cooked
chicken meat
1 celery heart, chopped
¼ cucumber, diced
100 g/4 oz smoked Westphalian
or Parma ham
Ravigote sauce (see below)

AMERICAN
¾–1 lb cooked
chicken meat
1 celery heart, chopped
¼ cucumber, diced
¼ lb smoked Westphalian
or Parma ham
Ravigote sauce (see below)

Cut the chicken into cubes and mix with the celery and cucumber. Cut the ham into Julienne strips and set aside half. Mix the rest into the salad.

Add the ravigote sauce and toss well. Turn into a serving dish and garnish with the remaining ham. *Serves 4*

Ravigote sauce

METRIC/IMPERIAL
2 tablespoons tarragon vinegar
1 teaspoon French mustard
1 teaspoon castor sugar
salt and freshly ground
black pepper
5 tablespoons salad oil
1 teaspoon finely chopped shallot
or spring onion
1 teaspoon chopped capers
1 teaspoon finely chopped gherkin
1 tablespoon chopped parsley
or chervil

AMERICAN
3 tablespoons tarragon vinegar
1 teaspoon French mustard
1 teaspoon sugar
salt and freshly ground
black pepper
6 tablespoons salad oil
1 teaspoon finely chopped shallot
or scallion
1 teaspoon chopped capers
1 teaspoon finely chopped gherkin
1 tablespoon chopped parsley
or chervil

Mix all the ingredients together and use to toss the Chicken and ham salad (see above).

Chicken and apple salad

METRIC/IMPERIAL	AMERICAN
4 red dessert apples	4 red dessert apples
juice of 1 lemon	juice of 1 lemon
1 head chicory	1 head Belgian endive
100 g/4 oz celery heart, chopped	$\frac{3}{4}$ cup chopped celery heart
50 g/2 oz stuffed olives, sliced	$\frac{1}{3}$ cup stuffed olives, sliced
50 g/2 oz flaked almonds	$\frac{1}{2}$ cup flaked almonds
350 g/12 oz cooked chicken meat	$\frac{3}{4}$ lb cooked chicken meat
1 small lettuce	1 small head lettuce
dressing:	*dressing:*
150 ml/$\frac{1}{4}$ pint natural yogurt	$\frac{2}{3}$ cup plain yogurt
4 tablespoons Mayonnaise	$\frac{2}{3}$ cups Mayonnaise
(page 100) or salad cream	(page 100) or salad cream
salt and freshly ground	salt and freshly ground
black pepper	black pepper

Core and chop three of the apples, but do not peel. Toss them in the lemon juice to prevent discoloration. Remove any damaged leaves from the chicory and cut the head into slices. Break up into rings. Mix together the apple, chicory, celery, olives and almonds. Cut the chicken into neat pieces and add to the salad.

To make the dressing, simply stir all the ingredients together. Mix thoroughly into the salad. Tear the lettuce into small pieces and use to line a salad bowl. Turn the salad into the lined bowl and garnish with the remaining apple, sliced or cut in wedges and tossed in lemon juice. Chill before serving. *Serves 4*

Lemon chicken and potato salad

METRIC/IMPERIAL	AMERICAN
350 g/12 oz cooked chicken meat	$\frac{3}{4}$ lb cooked chicken meat
3 lemons	3 lemons
3 tablespoons tarragon vinegar	$\frac{1}{4}$ cup tarragon vinegar
6 tablespoons salad oil	$\frac{1}{2}$ cup salad oil
salt and freshly ground	salt and freshly ground
black pepper	black pepper
1 bay leaf	1 bay leaf
1 sprig tarragon, marjoram	1 sprig tarragon, marjoram
or rosemary	or rosemary
150 ml/$\frac{1}{4}$ pint double cream	$\frac{2}{3}$ cup heavy cream
450 g/1 lb new potatoes, cooked	1 lb new potatoes, cooked
and sliced	and sliced
1 small cooked beetroot, chopped	1 small cooked beet, chopped
(optional)	(optional)
chopped mint, chervil or parsley	chopped mint, chervil or parsley
to garnish	to garnish

Cut the chicken into neat pieces. Squeeze the juice from two of the lemons and mix with the vinegar, oil, seasoning, bay leaf and herb for the marinade.

Turn the chicken into a bowl and pour over the marinade. Cut the remaining lemon in slices and spread over the top of the chicken. Leave for at least 2 hours, but preferably overnight.

When ready to serve, remove the chicken from the marinade and discard the herbs. Mix the cream into the marinade and adjust the seasoning. Place the potatoes in a serving dish and pour over some of the cream and marinade mixture. Sprinkle with a little of the chosen chopped herb for garnish and arrange the chicken on top. Add the beetroot if used and garnish with the slices of lemon and the rest of the chopped herbs. *Serves 4*

Coronation chicken

(Illustrated opposite)

This delightful buffet dish from Constance Spry was a first choice at many Coronation parties and has remained a favourite ever since. The chicken is best simmered, which also produces some good chicken stock. It can also be roasted.

The mayonnaise sauce is delicately flavoured with curry and apricot purée, which is best made with cooked dried apricots. If canned apricots are used, unless they are unsweetened, you will need extra lemon juice to counteract the sweetness.

METRIC/IMPERIAL	AMERICAN
1 cooked chicken	1 cooked chicken
1 tablespoon oil	1 tablespoon oil
1 small onion, chopped	1 small onion, chopped
1–2 teaspoons curry powder	1–2 teaspoons curry powder
2 teaspoons tomato purée	2 teaspoons tomato paste
6 tablespoons dry white wine	$\frac{1}{2}$ cup dry white wine
$4\frac{1}{2}$ tablespoons chicken stock	5 tablespoons chicken stock
or water	or water
salt and freshly ground	salt and freshly ground
black pepper	black pepper
1 teaspoon sugar	1 teaspoon sugar
2–3 teaspoons lemon juice	2–3 teaspoons lemon juice
300 ml/$\frac{1}{2}$ pint Mayonnaise	$1\frac{1}{4}$ cups Mayonnaise
(page 100)	(page 100)
3 tablespoons apricot purée	$\frac{1}{4}$ cup apricot purée
2–3 tablespoons double cream	$\frac{1}{4}$–$\frac{1}{3}$ cup heavy cream
garnish:	*garnish:*
sliced apricot and sprigs watercress	sliced apricot and sprigs watercress
or black and green grapes, halved	or black and green grapes, halved
and pipped and toasted flaked	and pipped and toasted flaked
almonds	almonds

Joint the chicken and discard the skin and bones. Cut the flesh into neat pieces and leave until cold. Heat the oil and fry the onion gently until soft. Add the curry powder and tomato purée and fry, stirring, for a further 3 minutes. Stir in the wine and stock or water and cook, uncovered, for about 10 minutes. Season to taste with salt, pepper, sugar and lemon juice. Cool thoroughly. Gradually stir the mixture into the mayonnaise and then add the apricot purée.

Lightly whip the cream and stir into the sauce. Adjust the seasoning. Mix in the chicken. Turn into a serving dish and chill. Serve garnished according to taste with a rice salad. *Serves 4*

Coronation chicken (see above)

Pineapple chicken salad

This refreshing salad makes an effective buffet dish. It can also be served in individual portions in scallop shells as a first course. A border of garden cress is an attractive garnish.

METRIC/IMPERIAL	AMERICAN
100 g/4 oz long-grain rice	$\frac{1}{2}$ cup long-grain rice
1 large fresh pineapple	1 large fresh pineapple
225 g/8 oz cooked chicken meat	$\frac{1}{2}$ lb cooked chicken meat
175 g/6 oz cooked green beans, chopped	$1\frac{1}{2}$ cups chopped cooked green beans
1 small celery heart, chopped	1 small celery heart, chopped
dressing:	*dressing:*
grated rind and juice of 1 orange	grated rind and juice of 1 orange
juice of 1 lime or lemon	juice of 1 lime or lemon
2 tablespoons chopped mint or tarragon	3 tablespoons chopped mint or tarragon
1 teaspoon castor sugar	1 teaspoon sugar
salt and freshly ground black pepper	salt and freshly ground black pepper
4 tablespoons salad oil	$\frac{1}{3}$ cup salad oil

Cook the rice in plenty of boiling salted water for 12 minutes or until just tender. Drain in a colander and cover with a dry tea cloth until dry and fluffy. Cut the pineapple in half lengthwise. Cut out the flesh, taking care to leave the skin and leaves intact. Remove the centre core and chop the flesh into small chunks. Mix with the rice.

Cut the chicken into small cubes and add to the pineapple and rice with the beans and celery heart.

Mix the orange rind and juice with the lime or lemon juice. Add the mint or tarragon, sugar and seasoning. Whisk in the oil. Add the salad and adjust the seasoning. Mix well and use to fill the pineapple halves. Chill well.

Serve in a bowl or a deep dish lined with crisp lettuce leaves. *Serves 4*

West Country chicken with cider (see page 66)

Bird in a pot

Soups

Chicken stock: Excellent stock and bouillon can be made with poultry. When a whole bird is boiled as described on page 57, the resulting liquor, well flavoured with its herbs and vegetables, makes a tasty and nourishing broth which can be served as a soup. The carcass from a jointed bird, together with the giblets, can be cooked into a strong bouillon or jellied stock, which makes a flavoursome base for sauces, soups and aspic jelly. The giblets, without the carcass, will produce sufficient stock to give a good flavour to gravies and sauces.

Giblet stock

To clean giblets: The giblets consist of the bird's neck, gizzard or crop, heart and liver. They must be carefully cleaned before using. The gizzard should be neatly slit round the curved outer edge and the inner sac, which contains semi-digested food, discarded. If the inner sac is broken, remove the outer skin and wash out the contents thoroughly. Remove the gall-bladder if it is still attached to the liver. If it has been broken in drawing the bird, cut off any liver that has been stained yellow as it will taste bitter. Remove any surplus fat from the heart and squeeze out any blood clots under cold running water.

METRIC/IMPERIAL	AMERICAN
1–2 sets giblets, cleaned	1–2 sets giblets, cleaned
1 bay leaf	1 bay leaf
1 sprig parsley	1 sprig parsley
1 shallot (optional)	1 shallot (optional)
8–10 peppercorns	8–10 peppercorns
salt to taste	salt to taste
300–600 ml/$\frac{1}{2}$–1 pint water	$1\frac{1}{4}$–$2\frac{1}{2}$ cups water

Put all the ingredients in a small pan, add the cold water. Cover and simmer for 20 minutes or until required.

Chicken stock or bouillon

METRIC/IMPERIAL

chicken carcass, skin and giblets
3–4 carrots
1 turnip
1 large onion
2–3 sticks celery
1 bay leaf
1 large sprig parsley
1 sprig rosemary
1 sprig thyme
6–8 peppercorns
1 teaspoon salt
2·25 litres/4 pints cold water

AMERICAN

chicken carcass, skin and giblets
3–4 carrots
1 turnip
1 large onion
2–3 stalks celery
1 bay leaf
1 large sprig parsley
1 sprig rosemary
1 sprig thyme
6–8 peppercorns
1 teaspoon salt
10 cups water

Wash the chicken carcass in cold water. Prepare and clean the giblets, discarding any fat from the skin. Put all in a large saucepan. Peel and chop the vegetables and add them to the pan with the herbs, peppercorns and salt. Cover with the water. Bring slowly to the boil and skim off the scum when it rises. Cover and simmer very gently for 1 hour for a quick stock, 2 hours for a strong bouillon. For a more concentrated bouillon, leave off the lid so that the stock reduces during cooking.

Strain, cool quickly and then remove the fat by passing pieces of absorbent or tissue paper across the surface of the stock.

Chicken aspic jelly

A packet of aspic crystals can be very convenient for glazing chicken mousse, galantine and chaudfroid dishes – see the Cold bird section. On the other hand, the more flavoursome home-made jelly is an essential ingredient for the Raised chicken pie (page 30).

For the pie, jellied chicken bouillon made from the carcass and giblets, reduced until it jells naturally and then melted and strained, may be used without further preparation. However, for dishes which require a crystal clear jelly, the bouillon must be cleared before setting by the addition of egg whites and shells and very lean beef, which contain the essential albumen.

METRIC/IMPERIAL	AMERICAN
1·15 litres/2 pints jellied chicken bouillon	5 cups jellied chicken bouillon
175 g/6 oz lean leg of beef, minced	$\frac{3}{4}$ cup ground lean beef shank
4 tablespoons dry sherry	$\frac{1}{3}$ cup dry sherry
2 egg whites	2 egg whites
2 egg shells	2 egg shells
salt and freshly ground black pepper	salt and freshly ground black pepper
lemon juice to taste	lemon juice to taste

Carefully remove any grease from the bouillon by straining it through a cold, wet cloth into an enamel-lined saucepan. Add the meat and sherry. Whip the egg whites to a soft froth and add them to the pan with the crushed egg shells. Continue whisking over a moderate heat until the bouillon comes to the boil. Stop whisking and allow the froth to rise to the top of the saucepan. Draw aside and leave the crust to settle, then boil up again slowly so the crust does not break. Scald a clean cloth and line a large strainer placed over a bowl. When the bouillon has settled for 7–10 minutes, pour into the strainer, holding back the frothy crust with a large draining spoon until the end, then allow it to slide into the strainer. Move the strainer to another bowl and pour the bouillon carefully through the frothy filter a second time. Season the liquid jelly and flavour to taste with the lemon juice.

Scots chicken and almond soup – Feather fowlie

This rich and satisfying soup, a favourite of Mary Queen of Scots, has a delicate flavour of almonds and cream.

METRIC/IMPERIAL	AMERICAN
1 small boiling chicken	1 small stewing chicken
2 medium onions	2 medium onions
1 turnip	1 turnip
1 parsnip	1 parsnip
3–4 carrots	3–4 carrots
3 sticks celery	3 stalks celery
1 bay leaf	1 bay leaf
1 sprig each parsley and thyme	1 sprig each parsley and thyme
10 peppercorns	10 peppercorns
salt	salt
50 g/2 oz ground almonds	$\frac{1}{2}$ cup ground almonds
3 tablespoons fresh white breadcrumbs	$\frac{1}{4}$ cup fresh soft bread crumbs
150 ml/$\frac{1}{4}$ pint double cream	$\frac{2}{3}$ cup heavy cream
2 tablespoons chopped chives or parsley to garnish	3 tablespoons chopped chives or parsley to garnish

Put the trussed fowl with the cleaned giblets in a large saucepan. Cover with cold water. Clean, peel and chop the vegetables and add with the herbs and seasonings to the pan. Bring to the boil quickly. Reduce the heat and skim carefully. Continue to simmer slowly for 2 hours or until the bird is very tender.

Lift the bird from the pan and remove the flesh from the bones. Put the meat in the blender. Strain the stock, set the giblets and herbs aside; add the vegetables to the blender with a little of the stock and make a purée. Alternatively, put the meat and vegetables through a fine mincer.

Return the purée to the saucepan, stir in the ground almonds and breadcrumbs and about 1·15 litres/2 pints (U.S. 5 cups) of the strained stock.

Simmer for 15–20 minutes. Mix a cup of soup into the cream and stir this into the soup. Heat without boiling and serve sprinkled with snipped chives or chopped parsley. *Serves 6–8*

Avgolemono

This traditional Greek chicken and lemon soup is very simple to make. It has a pleasant refreshing taste so it is an attractive choice for summer days.

METRIC/IMPERIAL	AMERICAN
1·15 litres/2 pints Chicken stock (page 55)	5 cups Chicken stock (page 55)
50 g/2 oz rice	6 tablespoons rice
1 large or 2 small lemons	1 large or 2 small lemons
2 eggs	2 eggs
chopped mint to garnish	chopped mint to garnish

Strain the chicken stock and bring to the boil. Add the rice and cook for 20 minutes. Squeeze the juice from the lemons and beat together with the eggs. Gradually blend in a cupful of chicken stock, then stir this mixture back into the pan. Heat the soup but do not allow it to boil. Serve sprinkled with chopped mint. *Serves 6*

Cream of chicken soup

This creamy soup is equally suitable for a family meal or a lunch or dinner party.

METRIC/IMPERIAL	AMERICAN
600 ml/1 pint Chicken stock (page 55)	2½ cups Chicken stock (page 55)
600 ml/1 pint Blanquette sauce (page 93)	2½ cups Blanquette sauce (page 93)
1 tablespoon chopped chives	1 tablespoon chopped chives
2 tablespoons chopped parsley	3 tablespoons chopped parsley
150 ml/¼ pint cream	⅔ cup cream
lemon juice to taste	lemon juice to taste
salt and freshly ground black pepper	salt and freshly ground black pepper
croûtons to garnish	croûtons to garnish

Remove any bones and giblets from the stock, but leave in the vegetables. Heat the blanquette sauce in a large pan and gradually blend in the chicken stock. Bring to the simmer and cook gently for 30 minutes stirring frequently.

Strain into a large bowl. Push the vegetables through a sieve with a wooden spoon or put into a blender with a little stock to make a purée. Put the soup and vegetable purée back into the pan, add the chives and parsley and bring to the simmer. Mix a little soup into the cream and stir this mixture into the soup. Heat through, but do not boil. Adjust the seasoning and sharpen to taste with lemon juice.

Serve hot with bread croûtons, crisply fried in butter. *Serves 6–8*

Boiled fowl

Birds which are too old to roast, grill or fry can be made into a variety of attractive dishes by simmering slowly in a well-seasoned stock, flavoured with vegetables and herbs.

The surplus fat around the vent and any eggs should first be removed and the breast rubbed with lemon juice to keep it white. Truss the bird as for roasting (page 13). If it is not much over a year old it will be cooked in about $1\frac{1}{4}$ hours, but if it is a large farmyard fowl weighing about 2·25 kg/5 lb, it will take 2 hours or more.

Cock-a-leekie

This traditional Scottish crofter's dish is cooked like Boiled chicken with rice (page 62) but using 450 g/1 lb leeks instead of carrots, pearl barley instead of rice and a few prunes for flavour. Sometimes the flesh is removed from the bones when the fowl is cooked and served in the soup like French pot-au-feu, but usually the soup and chicken are served separately with a lemon or parsley sauce.

Boiley-bakey chicken

This is a less expensive alternative to roast chicken.

Boil the bird in a well-flavoured stock until nearly tender, but not completely cooked, and remove from the pot. Drain well and pat the outside dry with absorbent paper. Put 50–75 g/2–3 oz (U.S. 4–6 tablespoons) lard in a roasting pan and heat it in a hot oven (220°C, 425°F, Gas Mark 7). Put the bird in the oven and baste it with the hot fat. Roast for 20–30 minutes, according to size, basting frequently, until golden brown and the legs are tender.

Chipolata sausages can be roasted around the bird to make a tasty garnish.

Petite marmite

(Illustrated on page 86)

This French soup is named after the little brown pots, like individual casseroles, in which it is traditionally served. The vegetables can be cut in fine Julienne strips, shredded or chopped.

METRIC/IMPERIAL	AMERICAN
1·15 litres/2 pints Chicken stock (page 55)	5 cups Chicken stock (page 55)
1 leek	1 leek
2 tablespoons shredded or chopped carrot	3 tablespoons shredded or chopped carrot
2 tablespoons shredded or chopped young turnip	3 tablespoons shredded or chopped young turnip
2 tablespoons shredded cabbage heart	3 tablespoons shredded cabbage heart
2 tablespoons shredded or chopped cooked chicken meat	3 tablespoons shredded or chopped cooked chicken meat
salt and freshly ground black pepper	salt and freshly ground black pepper
chopped parsley and croûtons to garnish	chopped parsley and croûtons to garnish

Strain the chicken stock and skim off the fat. Cut off the white part of the leek, clean it and slice it finely. Bring the stock to the boil and add the leek, carrot, turnip and cabbage. Simmer for 15 minutes, add the shredded chicken and cook for a further 5 minutes. Adjust the seasoning and garnish with chopped parsley.

Serve in a tureen or individual soup bowls with croûtons or a bowl of grated Parmesan cheese. *Serves 6–8*

Boiled chicken with rice and parsley sauce

METRIC/IMPERIAL	AMERICAN
1 (1·75–2·25-kg/4–5-lb) boiling chicken	1 (4–5-lb) stewing chicken
lemon juice	lemon juice
12 button onions, peeled	12 tiny onions, peeled
2–3 sticks celery, chopped	2–3 stalks celery, chopped
450 g/1 lb small carrots, scraped	1 lb small carrots, scraped
2 bay leaves	2 bay leaves
1 large sprig parsley	1 large sprig parsley
1 sprig thyme or rosemary	1 sprig thyme or rosemary
8 peppercorns	8 peppercorns
salt	salt
100 g/4 oz belly pork, salted or fresh	$\frac{1}{4}$ lb salt pork
350 g/12 oz long-grain rice	$1\frac{2}{3}$ cups long-grain rice
450 ml/$\frac{3}{4}$ pint Parsley sauce (page 94)	2 cups Parsley sauce (page 94)
chopped parsley to garnish	chopped parsley to garnish

Rub the chicken with lemon juice before boiling. Half-fill a large saucepan with water, add the vegetables, herbs and seasoning. Bring to the boil. Put in the giblets and chicken, breast uppermost, and make sure the legs are covered by water. Remove the rind from the pork, cut into 5-cm/2-inch chunks and add to the pot. Cover and simmer very gently for 30 minutes, then turn the bird on one side for 20 minutes, and then on the other side. Continue simmering until the legs are tender. When cooked, lift out of the pot, cover with a cloth and keep warm.

Strain the stock into a cold bowl and set aside the pork and vegetables. Skim off as much fat as possible and remove the remainder with absorbent or tissue paper. Pour the stock back into the saucepan, retaining 300 ml/$\frac{1}{2}$ pint (U.S. $1\frac{1}{4}$ cups) for the sauce, bring to the boil and add the rice. Cook for 12–14 minutes until only just tender, then strain into a colander or sieve and cover with a dry cloth to keep warm.

Meanwhile, make the parsley sauce using 300 ml/$\frac{1}{2}$ pint (U.S. $1\frac{1}{4}$ cups) of the strained chicken stock.

To serve, place the chicken on a carving dish with the pieces of pork and onions and garnish with parsley. Slice the carrots, toss in butter with cooked peas or chopped green beans and place on a warmed vegetable dish. Serve the rice and parsley sauce in separate bowls. *Serves 6–8*

Blanquette of chicken

This French dish is a party version of Boiled chicken with rice (page 62). It is a carefree dish for the cook/hostess as it can easily be prepared in advance and all you need is 15 minutes to cook the rice for the border.

METRIC/IMPERIAL	AMERICAN
1 small boiling chicken	1 small stewing chicken
1 onion	1 onion
3–4 carrots, sliced	3–4 carrots, sliced
1 stick celery	1 stalk celery
1 bay leaf	1 bay leaf
1 large sprig parsley	1 large sprig parsley
salt and freshly ground black pepper	salt and freshly ground black pepper
600 ml/1 pint Blanquette sauce (page 93)	$2\frac{1}{2}$ cups Blanquette sauce (page 93)
225 g/8 oz long-grain rice	1 cup long-grain rice
mushroom caps and parsley sprigs to garnish	mushroom caps and parsley sprigs to garnish

Prepare the fowl for boiling (page 60). If you are in a hurry, the bird may be cut into joints and these will cook very much more quickly than the whole bird. Put in a saucepan with the vegetables, herbs and seasoning, and cover with hot water. Bring rapidly to the boil, then lower the heat. Cover and simmer very gently until the legs are tender.

Lift out the chicken, skin and divide into joints if whole. Strain the stock and measure 300 ml/$\frac{1}{2}$ pint (U.S. $1\frac{1}{4}$ cups). Use to make the blanquette sauce. When the sauce is ready, add the chicken joints and heat through. Adjust the seasoning.

Meanwhile cook the rice in the remaining stock for 12 minutes or until tender. Strain into a colander and dry under a cloth.

Arrange the rice in a border around a warmed serving dish and put the chicken and sauce in the centre. Garnish the border with carrot slices from the stock, fried mushroom caps and parsley sprigs. *Serves 4*

Casseroled or sautéed bird

Casserole cooking, long a favourite method in peasant families throughout Europe, has become increasingly popular.

It is particularly suitable for tenderising older birds and is a very convenient method for the cook who is a single-handed hostess, or has a very unpunctual family, as food can be kept warm while waiting without spoiling.

Earthenware and ovenproof glass are inexpensive, but they cannot be used on a naked flame. Some of them can be put on a special type of heat-diffusing mat over a very low heat, but they are really safest in the oven. Meat or poultry, which has to be browned before liquid is added, must be cooked in a frying pan and then transferred to the casserole.

Flameproof casseroles made of 'rocket glass' or metal are more expensive, but are also much more versatile, being three pots in one. They can be used on top of the stove to sauté meat and make sauces, then left to simmer gently over a low heat or transferred to a slow oven. Many are so attractively finished that they can be placed on the table for serving. This all saves time and labour, especially if the lining is a non-stick one.

Pot-roasting is suitable for cooking a bird whole, and a flameproof, deep, oval casserole is the best shape to use. The chicken is first browned all over in hot fat, with one or two whole onions spiked with cloves. A glass of wine or stock is then added with herbs and seasoning. A close-fitting lid is put on and the bird left to cook very slowly over a low heat, allowing about 30 minutes per 0·5 kg/ 1 lb. When the bird is cooked, the onion is discarded, surplus fat removed from the casserole and the juices served as gravy, which may be slightly thickened and extended with stock as in oven-roasting.

Casseroled bird in sauce: for these dishes the bird is usually divided into joints which are first sautéed in hot fat before vegetables and liquid are added. A flameproof casserole, which is fairly shallow and wide enough to fry several joints, is best.

Sauté pans are wide shallow saucepans with a lid, and are also suitable for cooking jointed birds. They are aluminium, stainless steel or iron and the best are lined with enamel or a non-stick finish. If the pan has a long handle, cooking will have to be confined to the top of the stove, but if it has small heatproof handles, cooking can be completed in the oven.

In addition to the following recipes, other interesting casserole dishes are found in the Foreign and exotic birds section (page 79).

To joint a chicken

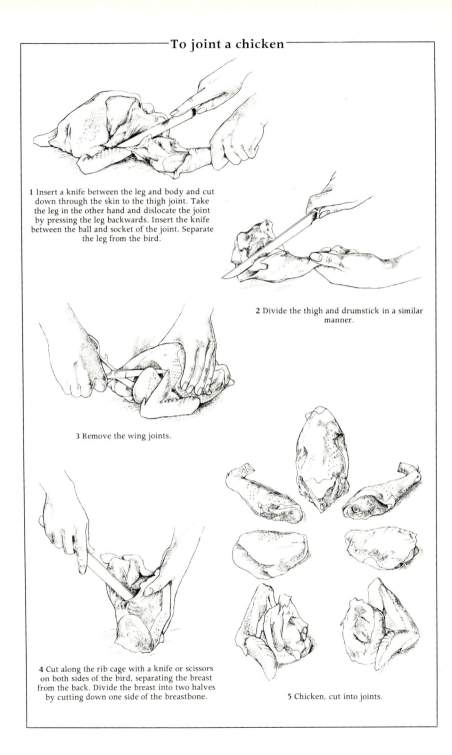

1 Insert a knife between the leg and body and cut down through the skin to the thigh joint. Take the leg in the other hand and dislocate the joint by pressing the leg backwards. Insert the knife between the ball and socket of the joint. Separate the leg from the bird.

2 Divide the thigh and drumstick in a similar manner.

3 Remove the wing joints.

4 Cut along the rib cage with a knife or scissors on both sides of the bird, separating the breast from the back. Divide the breast into two halves by cutting down one side of the breastbone.

5 Chicken, cut into joints.

West Country chicken with cider

(Illustrated on page 52)

This is a typical West Country dish with its cider, cream and apples. The meat from the carcass and giblets together with stock will make a tasty risotto (page 112) which can be served the next day.

METRIC/IMPERIAL	AMERICAN
1 oven-ready chicken, about	1 ready-to-cook chicken, about
1·75 kg/3½ lb	3½ lb
stock:	*stock:*
1 small onion	1 small onion
1 stick celery	1 stalk celery
1 bay leaf	1 bay leaf
1 sprig parsley	1 sprig parsley
salt	salt
few peppercorns	few peppercorns
sauce:	*sauce:*
50 g/2 oz flour	½ cup flour
75 g/3 oz unsalted butter	6 tablespoons sweet butter
1 large onion, thinly sliced	1 large onion, thinly sliced
2 sticks celery, chopped	2 stalks celery, chopped
1 large or 2 small cooking apples	1 large or 2 small baking apples
150 ml/¼ pint cider	⅔ cup cider
300 ml/½ pint giblet stock	1¼ cups giblet stock
2–4 tablespoons double cream	¼–⅓ cup heavy cream
salt and freshly ground	salt and freshly ground
black pepper	black pepper
garnish:	*garnish:*
apple rings and celery leaves or	apple rings and celery leaves or
cooked young carrots,	cooked young carrots,
button onions and peas	button onions and peas

Cut the chicken into joints (page 65) and remove the skin. Put the carcass and giblets in a saucepan with all the stock ingredients, cover with water and simmer gently with a lid on until the stock is needed.

Use the flour for the sauce to coat the chicken joints. Pat off any surplus. Heat two-thirds of the butter in a flameproof casserole or sauté pan and fry the joints briskly until browned all over. Remove the chicken, add the onion and celery to the pan and fry gently until soft.

Peel, core and roughly chop the apples, add to the pan and fry until well buttered. Take the pan from the heat and stir in the flour left from coating to absorb the fat. Gradually stir in the cider and giblet stock. Bring to simmering point, add the chicken and a little more stock if necessary to cover the joints. Cover and simmer gently for 30 minutes or until the chicken is tender.

Remove the joints to a heated serving plate and keep warm. Cook the sauce, uncovered for 5 minutes or until slightly thickened. Mix 2–3 tablespoons of the sauce into the cream and stir into the sauce in the pan. Adjust the seasoning. Pour the sauce over the joints and garnish with apple rings fried in the remaining butter until golden and tufts of celery leaves. In summer use young carrots, button onions, and peas tossed in the butter as a garnish. *Serves 4*

Autumn casserole of chicken

This is an ideal dish to make when the orchards and markets are full of colourful autumn fruit.

METRIC/IMPERIAL	AMERICAN
1 roasting chicken, about	1 roaster chicken, about
1·5 kg/3 lb	3 lb
1 bay leaf	1 bay leaf
1 sprig parsley	1 sprig parsley
salt and freshly ground	salt and freshly ground
black pepper	black pepper
2 tablespoons flour	3 tablespoons flour
50 g/2 oz butter or margarine	$\frac{1}{4}$ cup butter or margarine
2 medium onions, chopped	2 medium onions, chopped
$\frac{1}{4}$ teaspoon powdered saffron	$\frac{1}{4}$ teaspoon powdered saffron
1 teaspoon crushed coriander	1 teaspoon crushed coriander
seed	seed
3 knobs stem ginger, chopped	3 knobs stem ginger, chopped
225 g/8 oz dessert apples	$\frac{1}{2}$ lb dessert apples
450 g/1 lb Conference pears	1 lb Conference pears
225 g/8 oz red plums	$\frac{1}{2}$ lb red plums
2 tablespoons ginger syrup	3 tablespoons ginger syrup
chopped chervil or parsley	chopped chervil or parsley
to garnish	to garnish

Joint and skin the chicken (page 65) and cook the carcass and giblets in water to cover with the bay leaf, parsley and seasoning to make a stock. Coat the joints with the flour and pat off any surplus. Heat the butter in a flameproof casserole and fry the joints until golden on both sides. Remove from the casserole and fry the onion until softened. Replace the chicken in the casserole and add enough strained stock to cover the joints. Add the saffron, coriander, ginger and seasoning. Cover and simmer for 20 minutes.

Peel, core and slice the apples and pears. Cut the plums around the crease, twist the halves apart and remove the stones. Add the fruit and the ginger syrup to the casserole and simmer for about 25 minutes until the chicken is tender.

Sprinkle with chervil or parsley and serve with baked jacket potatoes. *Serves 4*

Coq au vin de Bourgogne

This is one of the chicken dishes which most often appears on restaurant menus but, sadly, frequently turns out to be indifferently stewed chicken instead of the rich Burgundian casserole of its country of origin. In this traditional recipe, the bird is cooked whole, but it may be jointed if preferred. If pickled pork is not available, green streaky bacon may be used.

METRIC/IMPERIAL	AMERICAN
giblet stock ingredients (page 54)	giblet stock ingredients (page 54)
75 g/3 oz unsalted butter	6 tablespoons sweet butter
100 g/4 oz pickled belly pork, diced	$\frac{1}{4}$ lb salt pork, diced
12 button onions	12 tiny onions
175–225 g/6–8 oz button mushrooms	$1\frac{1}{2}$–2 cups mushrooms
1 young cockerel or chicken	1 broiler-fryer chicken
1 tablespoon brandy	1 tablespoon brandy
$\frac{1}{2}$–$\frac{3}{4}$ bottle Burgundy or dry red wine	$\frac{1}{2}$–$\frac{3}{4}$ bottle Burgundy or dry red wine
1 bouquet garni	1 bouquet garni
1 clove garlic	1 clove garlic
salt and freshly ground black pepper	salt and freshly ground black pepper
chopped parsley and croûtons to garnish	chopped parsley and croûtons to garnish
beurre manié:	*beurre manié:*
25 g/1 oz butter	2 tablespoons butter
25 g/1 oz flour	$\frac{1}{4}$ cup flour

Put the giblet stock ingredients on to cook and reduce into a well-flavoured bouillon.

Heat the butter in a flameproof casserole with the pickled pork and cook gently until the fat runs. Add the peeled onions and fry until golden. Wash and add the mushrooms, and cook for a few minutes. Remove all from the pan and brown the bird all over, turning carefully. Spoon out surplus fat. Warm the brandy in a tiny saucepan or a large spoon, set alight and pour it flaming over the bird. Move the bird about until the flames subside, then pour in the wine.

Add the herbs with the pressed garlic, onions and mushrooms. Strain in sufficient giblet stock so that the bird is half covered. Put on the lid and simmer very gently until the legs are tender, turning the bird from time to time.

When cooked, remove the bird to a heated serving dish. Surround with the onions and mushrooms and keep warm.

Leave the sauce boiling briskly, uncovered, to reduce. Meanwhile, cream together the butter and flour and roll into little balls of *beurre manié*. Turn the heat down under the casserole, remove the bouquet garni and gradually stir in the *beurre manié* until the sauce is of the desired consistency. Season and pour into a warmed sauce boat.

Sprinkle the chicken with chopped parsley and garnish with croûtons. *Serves 4*

Serving suggestions: The bird may be jointed, before serving, and the sauce poured over.

Accompany with creamed or duchesse potatoes and Brussels sprouts, or runner beans chopped French-style, not sliced.

Scalloped potatoes

Well butter a shallow gratin dish and fill with layers of sliced potatoes (450 g/ 1 lb), seasoned with salt and pepper and sprinkled with finely chopped onion and grated cheese. Beat an egg into 300 ml/½ pint (U.S. 1¼ cups) milk and pour this over the potatoes. Dot the top layer of grated cheese with butter and bake in a moderate oven (160°C, 325°F, Gas Mark 3) for 1½ hours or until cooked and golden.

Flemish chicken with chicory and prunes

The Belgians are great growers of chicory, which is often called Belgian endive, as in French its name is *endive*. Confusion can be caused by the fact that the curly salad vegetable called endive in English-speaking countries, is known as chicory on the Continent. No matter what it is called, it is equally good raw in a salad or cooked as in this recipe, when its slightly sharp taste is softened by the sweetness of the prunes.

METRIC/IMPERIAL	AMERICAN
1 (1·25-kg/2½-lb) chicken	1 (2½-lb) chicken
4 medium heads chicory	4 medium heads Belgian endive
225 g/8 oz ripe tomatoes	½ lb ripe tomatoes
25 g/1 oz butter	2 tablespoons butter
1 tablespoon olive oil	1 tablespoon olive oil
1 medium onion, sliced	1 medium onion, sliced
50 g/2 oz belly pork or bacon	2 oz salt pork or bacon
3–4 tablespoons sherry	4–5 tablespoons sherry
¼ teaspoon dried mixed herbs	¼ teaspoon dried mixed herbs
salt and freshly ground	salt and freshly ground
black pepper	black pepper
8 large prunes	8 large prunes
450 ml/¾ pint chicken stock	2 cups chicken stock
4 tablespoons cream (optional)	⅓ cup cream (optional)

Joint the bird (page 65) and put the carcass and giblets to cook to make stock (page 54).

Trim the base of the chicory heads and remove any discoloured leaves. Skin the tomatoes and chop roughly. Heat the butter and oil in a flameproof casserole and fry the chicory until golden brown all over. Remove them and brown the chicken joints. Remove and fry the onion and pork or bacon until just colouring. Mix in the tomatoes, sherry, herbs and seasoning. Add the chicken, chicory and prunes and sufficient chicken stock to almost cover the bird. Cover and simmer gently on top of the stove or in a moderate oven (160°C, 325°F, Gas Mark 3) for 1½ hours until tender.

Arrange the chicken joints, chicory heads and stoned prunes in a warmed serving dish. If using cream, stir this into the casserole. Adjust the seasoning, heat through and pour over the joints. Serve with Scalloped potatoes (page 69) which cook conveniently in the oven at the same time as the casserole. *Serves 4*

Chicken with lemon and artichokes

The fresh lemons combined with the subtle flavour of the artichokes give this dish its unique appeal. Unless you live in a country where fresh globe artichokes are prolific and cheap, the canned *fonds* (bottoms) may be preferred. Sometimes canned hearts are easier to come by and may be substituted if necessary.

METRIC/IMPERIAL	AMERICAN
1 (1·5-kg/3½-lb) roasting chicken	1 (3½-lb) roaster chicken
50 g/2 oz seasoned flour	½ cup seasoned flour
50 g/2 oz butter	¼ cup butter
1 tablespoon chopped onion	1 tablespoon chopped onion
4 fresh artichoke bottoms or	4 fresh artichoke bottoms or
1 (350-g/12-oz) can artichoke bottoms	1 (12-oz) can artichoke bottoms
6 tablespoons white wine	½ cup white wine
1 large or 2 small lemons	1 large or 2 small lemons
450 ml/¾ pint giblet stock or bouillon	2 cups giblet stock or bouillon
150 ml/¼ pint double cream	⅔ cup heavy cream
salt and freshly ground black pepper	salt and freshly ground black pepper

Joint the chicken (page 65) and put the carcass and giblets to cook to make stock (page 54).

Coat the chicken with flour. Pat off surplus and fry in a flameproof casserole in hot butter, turning once, until golden brown. Add the onion and fresh artichoke bottoms – halved if they are large – and the wine. (If using canned artichokes, add here with the liquor from the can and reduce the quantity of giblet stock accordingly.) Grate the zest from 1 small or half a large lemon and add to the pan with the juice. Pour in sufficient stock or bouillon to cover the chicken joints. Put on the lid and simmer very gently for 40 minutes or until the legs are tender.

Mix a few tablespoons of sauce with the cream and stir this into the pan. Adjust the seasoning and add more lemon juice if liked.

Heat through and garnish with lemon butterflies or zest, and serve with new potatoes or noodles tossed with the butter and fresh parsley. *Serves 4*

Chicken fricassée with soured cream sauce

This fricassée can also be made with double cream and extra lemon juice instead of soured cream. The fleurons are little puff pastry crescents made from pastry trimmings and glazed with beaten egg. Alternatively, triangular fried bread croûtons may be substituted.

METRIC/IMPERIAL	AMERICAN
1 oven-ready chicken, about 1·5 kg/3 lb	1 ready-to-cook chicken, about 3 lb
2 tablespoons flour	3 tablespoons flour
50 g/2 oz butter or margarine	$\frac{1}{4}$ cup butter or margarine
2 medium onions, sliced	2 medium onions, sliced
2–3 young carrots, sliced	2–3 young carrots, sliced
1 tablespoon finely chopped parsley or chervil	1 tablespoon finely chopped parsley or chervil
pinch of dried thyme	dash of dried thyme
salt and freshly ground black pepper	salt and freshly ground black pepper
1 (142-ml/5-fl oz) carton soured cream	1 (5-fl oz) carton dairy sour cream
2 egg yolks	2 egg yolks
lemon juice to taste	lemon juice to taste
garnish:	*garnish:*
fleurons or croûtons	fleurons or croûtons
few sprigs parsley or chervil	few sprigs parsley or chervil

Joint and skin the chicken (page 65) and boil up the carcass to make stock. Coat the joints with the flour, patting off the surplus. Heat the butter or margarine in a flameproof casserole or sauté pan and fry the chicken until golden all over. Remove the chicken and fry the onion until soft but not coloured. Return the chicken to the casserole and add enough stock to cover the joints. Add the carrot and parsley or chervil, thyme and seasoning. Cover and simmer or cook in a moderate oven (160°C, 325°F, Gas Mark 3) until tender, about 40 minutes.

Remove the chicken and cut the meat off the bone. Cut in neat pieces. Meanwhile, reduce the liquid by about one-third by brisk boiling.

Beat the soured cream and egg yolks together and stir with about half a cup of the cooling liquid. Stir this back into the casserole and cook very gently, stirring until thickened, but do not boil. Season and add lemon juice to taste. Stir in the chicken meat and heat through. Garnish with hot fleurons or croûtons and parsley or chervil. Serve with buttered baby carrots and peas. *Serves 4*

Poulet Jacqueline

This is a dish which is quickly made for the unexpected guest if boned chicken breasts or fillet are used.

METRIC/IMPERIAL	AMERICAN
4 large chicken breasts or	4 large chicken breasts or
8 fillets	8 fillets
2 tablespoons seasoned flour	3 tablespoons seasoned flour
75 g/3 oz butter	6 tablespoons butter
3 tablespoons port or Madeira	$\frac{1}{4}$ cup port or Madeira
300 ml/$\frac{1}{2}$ pint chicken stock	$1\frac{1}{4}$ cups chicken stock
salt and freshly ground	salt and freshly ground
black pepper	black pepper
150 ml/$\frac{1}{4}$ pint cream	$\frac{2}{3}$ cup cream
lemon juice to taste	lemon juice to taste
3 dessert apples	3 dessert apples
1–2 tablespoons flaked almonds,	1–3 tablespoons flaked almonds,
toasted	toasted

Fillet the breasts off the bone, separate each one into two and coat with seasoned flour. Melt half the butter in a flameproof casserole and fry the chicken until golden all over. Add the port or Madeira and boil for 1–2 minutes. Pour in enough stock to just cover the chicken. Season, cover and simmer gently for 25 minutes or until tender. Remove the chicken to a warm serving dish and reduce the liquid by half by brisk boiling. Mix the cream with half a cup of the liquid and stir back into the remaining liquid. Add lemon juice and seasoning to taste. Heat but do not boil.

Peel, core and slice the apples. Heat the remaining butter in a separate pan and fry the apple slices until golden on both sides.

Arrange the chicken on a heated serving dish in alternate rows with the apple. Pour over the sauce and scatter the almonds on top. Serve at once. *Serves 4*

Poulet Guizot

This is a nice, easy dish to prepare and cook. It can be made in advance and reheated. A very tasty and less expensive version can be made by using sliced Bramley apples instead of mushrooms and cider instead of wine, with crushed coriander to replace the herbs.

METRIC/IMPERIAL	AMERICAN
1 oven-ready chicken, about 1·25 kg/2½ lb or 4 chicken joints	1 ready-to-cook chicken, about 2½ lb or 4 chicken joints
50 g/2 oz butter	¼ cup butter
225 g/8 oz mushrooms, sliced	½ lb mushrooms, sliced
salt and freshly ground black pepper	salt and freshly ground black pepper
225 g/8 oz onions, chopped	½ lb onions, chopped
pinch of dried oregano or thyme	dash of dried oregano or thyme
50 g/2 oz crisp breadcrumbs	½ cup crisp bread crumbs
50 g/2 oz cheese, grated	½ cup grated cheese
175 ml/6 fl oz dry white wine	¾ cup dry white wine
50 g/2 oz even-sized mushroom caps to garnish	½ cup even-sized mushroom caps to garnish

Joint and skin the chicken (page 65) and separate the drumsticks from the thighs. Cut each breast across into two portions – poultry shears will make this easier. Use some of the butter to grease a casserole or gratin dish. Cover the base of the dish with the mushrooms, season and add the onion. Sprinkle the herbs over the onion and arrange the chicken on top. Season well. Mix the breadcrumbs with the cheese and use to cover the chicken. Pour in enough wine to come half-way up the joints. Cook in a moderately hot oven (200°C, 400°F, Gas Mark 6) for about 1 hour or until tender and the top crisp. If it browns too much, place a piece of foil on top. Serve with baked jacket potatoes or minted new potatoes and sugar peas or beans. *Serves 4*

Chicken livers de luxe

Nowadays chicken livers can conveniently be bought in packs of 225 g/8 oz and 450 g/1 lb.

The livers should always be carefully cleaned and never overcooked, or these tender morsels will become hard.

Chicken liver kebabs

METRIC/IMPERIAL	AMERICAN
For each skewer:	*For each skewer:*
1 chicken liver, cleaned	1 chicken liver, cleaned
1 tablespoon butter	1 tablespoon butter
1–2 bacon rolls	1–2 bacon rolls
2 mushroom caps	2 mushroom caps
1 wedge green pepper	1 wedge green pepper
1–2 cocktail sausages	1–2 cocktail sausages
oil for brushing	oil for brushing
salt and freshly ground	salt and freshly ground
black pepper	black pepper
dried mixed herbs	dried mixed herbs

Sauté the halved chicken liver in butter until just stiffened. Thread the ingredients on to the skewer, alternating the colours. Brush with oil, season well and sprinkle with herbs (or baste with Barbecue sauce, page 96). Grill on the stove or over a charcoal grill, turning frequently for about 10 minutes. *Serves 1*

Variation: Small chunks of chicken meat can be used instead of livers. (Illustrated on page 104.)

Button onions, mushroom caps and wedges of pineapple are attractive additions to the skewers.

Chicken liver crostini

METRIC/IMPERIAL	AMERICAN
225 g/8 oz chicken livers	$\frac{1}{2}$ lb chicken livers
40 g/1$\frac{1}{2}$ oz butter	3 tablespoons butter
100 g/4 oz ham, diced	$\frac{1}{2}$ cup diced cooked ham
2–3 tablespoons seasoned flour	3–4 tablespoons seasoned flour
2 tablespoons sherry	3 tablespoons sherry
4 tablespoons chicken stock	$\frac{1}{3}$ cup chicken stock
4 slices white bread	4 slices white bread
butter or oil	butter or oil
4 tablespoons cream	$\frac{1}{3}$ cup cream
salt and freshly ground	salt and freshly ground
black pepper	black pepper
lemon juice to taste	lemon juice to taste
grated lemon rind and chopped	grated lemon rind and chopped
parsley to garnish	parsley to garnish

Cut the cleaned chicken livers into neat pieces. Heat the butter in a saucepan and fry the ham quickly. Coat each piece of chicken liver in the seasoned flour, add to the pan and fry for 2–3 minutes until stiffened. Add the sherry and stock and cook gently for 8–10 minutes.

Meanwhile, cut a round out of each bread slice and fry quickly on both sides in the hot butter or oil in a frying pan. Drain on soft paper before placing on serving dishes. Add the cream to the livers, season and sharpen to taste with lemon. Pile on to the croûtes, sprinkle with grated lemon rind and parsley and serve at once. *Serves 4*

Chicken livers with vermouth and orange

METRIC/IMPERIAL	AMERICAN
225 g/8 oz chicken livers	$\frac{1}{2}$ lb chicken livers
50 g/2 oz butter	$\frac{1}{4}$ cup butter
50 g/2 oz button mushrooms, sliced	$\frac{1}{2}$ cup mushrooms, sliced
1 small onion, chopped	1 small onion, chopped
1 tablespoon seasoned flour	1 tablespoon seasoned flour
3 tablespoons vermouth	$\frac{1}{4}$ cup vermouth
grated rind and juice of 1 orange	grated rind and juice of 1 orange
lemon juice to taste	lemon juice to taste
salt and freshly ground black pepper	salt and freshly ground black pepper
450 g/1 lb mashed or duchesse potato	1 lb mashed or duchesse potato

Trim and halve the chicken livers. Melt the butter in a frying pan and fry the mushrooms and onion until just turning golden. Toss the liver in the seasoned flour and add to the pan. Fry, stirring, for 5 minutes. Add the vermouth and bring to the boil. Boil for 1–2 minutes. Add 2 teaspoons of the orange rind and the juice. Season and add lemon juice to taste. Remove the liver and boil the sauce until slightly reduced. Adjust the seasoning and return the liver to the sauce. Line four ramekins with the potato, either using a piping bag or a fork. Spoon in the liver and sauce. Garnish with the remaining rind and serve at once.
Serves 4

Quick chicken liver pâté

(Illustrated on page 86)

METRIC/IMPERIAL	AMERICAN
450 g/1 lb chicken livers	1 lb chicken livers
50 g/2 oz butter	$\frac{1}{4}$ cup butter
1 tablespoon brandy	1 tablespoon brandy
1 tablespoon Madeira or	1 tablespoon Madeira or
sweet sherry	sweet sherry
pinch of dried thyme or	dash of dried thyme or
oregano	oregano
pinch of dried marjoram	dash of dried marjoram
1 clove garlic, crushed	1 clove garlic, crushed
salt and freshly ground	salt and freshly ground
black pepper	black pepper

Trim the livers and remove any parts which are discoloured by the gall bladder. Chop the liver roughly. Heat the butter and fry the liver for about 5 minutes, or longer if you prefer the liver well cooked. Mince finely or purée in a blender.

Add the brandy and Madeira to the pan and boil, scraping up the residue. Pour into the liver purée and mix in the herbs and garlic. Season well and press into an earthenware pot or ramekins. Refrigerate overnight. The pâté will be tastier if it is allowed to mature for 1–2 days. Serve with hot toast or crusty French bread and butter. *Serves 4*

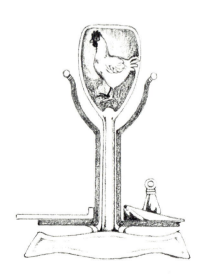

Foreign and exotic birds

Persian chicken

In the Middle East the average chicken works so hard to find its food, it is neither large nor plump; but recipes for cooking it often contain intriguing fruits and spices. For the following dish, the apricots, peaches and prunes should be soaked overnight and the liquor reserved.

METRIC/IMPERIAL	AMERICAN
2 poussins or 1 spring chicken	1 large or 2 small broiler chickens
2 tablespoons olive oil	3 tablespoons olive oil
2 medium onions, sliced	2 medium onions, sliced
50 g/2 oz dried apricots, soaked	$\frac{1}{3}$ cup dried apricots, soaked
50 g/2 oz dried peaches, soaked	$\frac{1}{3}$ cup dried peaches, soaked
4 stoned prunes, soaked	4 pitted prunes, soaked
grated rind and juice of 1 orange	grated rind and juice of 1 orange
1 sharp apple	1 sharp apple
2 tablespoons seedless raisins	3 tablespoons seeded raisins
$\frac{1}{4}$ teaspoon ground cinnamon	$\frac{1}{4}$ teaspoon ground cinnamon
pinch of ground ginger or saffron	dash of ground ginger or saffron
lemon juice to taste	lemon juice to taste
salt and freshly ground	salt and freshly ground
black pepper	black pepper

Truss the birds neatly (page 13). Heat the oil in a flameproof casserole. Brown the chickens all over and remove. Fry the onion gently until softened and just turning colour. Drain the apricots, peaches (quartered if large) and prunes and mix with the onions. Put back the chickens, add the orange rind and juice and sufficient liquor from the plumped fruits to come half-way up the birds. Add the apple, peeled and thickly sliced, raisins, cinnamon, ginger or saffron and lemon juice and seasoning to taste. Cover and simmer for 45 minutes or until tender, turning the birds from time to time. Sharpen the sauce with lemon juice and adjust the seasoning. *Serves 2*

Serving suggestions: Serve with fluffy boiled rice tossed with fried almond flakes or chopped walnuts, and with baked courgettes or aubergines.

Spiced Bangkok chicken

This Indo-Chinese dish is excellent for a buffet party as it is easy to serve at a help-yourself meal or fork luncheon, either as a main course or starter. The cumin and coriander seeds and peanut butter give the rice an intriguing flavour.

METRIC/IMPERIAL	AMERICAN
1 (1·75-kg/4-lb) dressed boiling chicken	1 (4-lb) ready-to-cook stewing chicken
450 g/1 lb onions	1 lb onions
1 bay leaf	1 bay leaf
1 sprig parsley	1 sprig parsley
salt and freshly ground black pepper	salt and freshly ground black pepper
450 g/1 lb long-grain rice	$2\frac{1}{3}$ cups long-grain rice
3 tablespoons vegetable oil	$\frac{1}{4}$ cup vegetable oil
2 tablespoons peanut butter	3 tablespoons peanut butter
$\frac{1}{2}$ teaspoon chilli powder	$\frac{1}{2}$ teaspoon chilli powder
175 g/6 oz cooked ham, diced	1 cup diced cooked ham
1 teaspoon cumin seeds	1 teaspoon cumin seeds
1 teaspoon coriander seeds	1 teaspoon coriander seeds
1 clove garlic	1 clove garlic
pinch of ground mace or grated nutmeg	dash of ground mace or grated nutmeg
cucumber, pineapple and lemon to garnish	cucumber, pineapple and lemon to garnish

Simmer the bird until tender with 1 onion, the bay leaf, parsley and salt and pepper to taste in water to cover. Lift out the bird and remove the meat from the bones.

Strain and reheat the stock, add the rice and cook until just tender, about 12 minutes. Drain through a colander and cover with a dry cloth.

Slice the remaining onions. Heat the oil in a large frying pan and fry the onions slowly until beginning to colour. Stir in the peanut butter, chilli powder, ham and chicken meat and then the rice, which should be dry and fluffy. Continue stirring and frying until the rice is slightly brown. Crush the cumin and coriander seeds and garlic and stir them, with the mace, into the rice. Season to taste with salt.

Pile on to a hot dish and garnish with sliced unpeeled cucumber and wedges of fresh pineapple and lemon. *Serves 6–8*

Serving suggestions: Surround the dish with little bowls containing various chutneys such as apricot, lemon and mango, and dishes of fried almonds, cashew nuts and toasted coconut.

Chicken moussaka

This Mediterranean dish is ideal for lunch or supper. It can be prepared in advance, frozen if required, and finished in a hot oven. It is important to drain the fried vegetables thoroughly or the moussaka will be oily.

METRIC/IMPERIAL	AMERICAN
400 g/14 oz aubergines	scant 1 lb eggplant
1 tablespoon salt	1 tablespoon salt
450 g/1 lb tomatoes	1 lb tomatoes
4 tablespoons oil	$\frac{1}{3}$ cup oil
75 g/3 oz margarine	6 tablespoons margarine
450 g/1 lb onions, sliced	1 lb onions, sliced
450 g/1 lb cooked chicken meat	1 lb cooked chicken meat
salt and freshly ground black pepper	salt and freshly ground black pepper
2 teaspoons sugar	2 teaspoons sugar
pinch of dried basil or marjoram	dash of dried basil or marjoram
300 ml/$\frac{1}{2}$ pint Cheese béchamel sauce, pouring consistency (page 94)	1$\frac{1}{4}$ cups Cheese béchamel sauce, pouring consistency (page 94)
50 g/2 oz cheese, grated	$\frac{1}{2}$ cup grated cheese

Wipe the aubergines and slice with a stainless knife in about 1-cm/$\frac{1}{2}$-inch slices. Spread on soft paper and sprinkle with salt. Peel and slice the tomatoes. Rinse the salt off the aubergines and dry the slices on soft paper. Heat the oil in a frying pan and fry the aubergines until golden on both sides, turning once. Fry only enough at a time to cover the pan. Drain the slices on soft paper. Add the margarine and fry the onion until just turning golden. Drain on soft paper. Spread a layer of onion over the base of a shallow flameproof casserole and season to taste. Cover with layers of chicken, tomato and aubergine, seasoning between layers with salt, pepper, sugar and herbs. Repeat the layers, ending with one of aubergine. Cover and cook in a moderately hot oven (190°C, 375°F, Gas Mark 5) for about 30 minutes until the juice runs from the onion and tomato. Pour over the hot cheese sauce and sprinkle with the grated cheese. Return to the oven to brown.

Serve with boiled potatoes tossed in butter with chopped mint or parsley.
Serves 4

Swiss chicken with cheese and white wine sauce

This is a favourite way to prepare chicken in Switzerland and in the Alpine regions of France and Austria. It is an excellent dish for the cook/hostess as it can be prepared in advance and then finished in a hot oven when required.

METRIC/IMPERIAL	AMERICAN
1 (1·25–1·5-kg/2½–3-lb) roasting chicken	1 (2½–3-lb) roaster chicken
ingredients for giblet stock (page 54)	ingredients for giblet stock (page 54)
75 g/3 oz butter	6 tablespoons butter
1 tablespoon chopped tarragon	1 tablespoon chopped tarragon
salt and freshly ground black pepper	salt and freshly ground black pepper
sauce:	*sauce:*
50 g/2 oz butter	¼ cup butter
50 g/2 oz flour	½ cup flour
150 ml/¼ pint giblet stock	⅔ cup giblet stock
300 ml/½ pint cream	1¼ cups cream
150 ml/¼ pint dry white wine	⅔ cup dry white wine
50 g/2 oz Gruyère or Emmenthal cheese, grated	½ cup grated Gruyère or Emmenthal cheese
2 teaspoons French mustard	2 teaspoons French mustard
salt and freshly ground black pepper	salt and freshly ground black pepper
topping:	*topping:*
4 tablespoons toasted breadcrumbs	⅓ cup toasted bread crumbs
2 tablespoons grated cheese	3 tablespoons grated cheese

Put the cleaned giblets in a pan with water and the stock ingredients. Boil until needed to make stock.

Cream the butter and tarragon together and season with salt and freshly ground black pepper. Place the chicken in a roasting pan and spread the butter over it. Roast in a moderately hot oven (200°C, 400°F, Gas Mark 6) for about 1 hour or until tender. Turn the chicken from time to time and baste with the tarragon butter. Alternatively, roast on a spit, basting frequently.

Meanwhile make the sauce. Melt the butter. Draw from the heat and stir in the flour. Gradually blend in the giblet stock and then the cream. Return to the heat and bring to the simmer, stirring continuously. When it begins to bubble, add the wine and continue cooking very gently for 4–5 minutes. Stir in the cheese and mustard and season to taste. Cover and keep warm. When the chicken is cooked, carve it into four portions.

Butter a warmed gratin dish and pour a layer of sauce over the base. Arrange the chicken pieces on top and coat with the remaining sauce. Sprinkle with toasted crumbs and cheese and trickle over some of the tarragon butter from the roasting tin. The dish can now be set aside and finished off when required. For immediate use, put in the top of a hot oven (220°C, 425°F, Gas Mark 7) and bake for 10–15 minutes until it has a bubbling golden crust. Alternatively, the dish may be finished under the grill. *Serves 4*

Serving suggestions: Accompany with sauté potatoes or buttered noodles, garnished with chopped parsley, and a salad.

Hungarian chicken paprikash

(Illustrated opposite)

This is a party version of the famous Hungarian chicken dish.

Paprika is a red pepper made from pimientos or sweet peppers and is not to be confused with the fiery hot cayenne pepper. It varies in strength and sufficient should be used to give the rosy pink sauce a distinctive paprika flavour.

METRIC/IMPERIAL	AMERICAN
1 (1·5-kg/3½-lb) roasting chicken	1 (3½-lb) roaster chicken
giblet stock ingredients	giblet stock ingredients
(page 54)	(page 54)
50 g/2 oz flour	½ cup flour
50 g/2 oz lard	¼ cup lard
225 g/8 oz mushrooms	2 cups mushrooms
1 medium onion, sliced	1 medium onion, sliced
300 ml/½ pint milk	1¼ cups milk
4 teaspoons tomato purée	4 teaspoons tomato paste
2–3 teaspoons paprika	2–3 teaspoons paprika pepper
2 teaspoons castor sugar	2 teaspoons sugar
150 ml/¼ pint single or soured cream	⅔ cup light or dairy sour cream
salt	salt
lemon juice to taste	lemon juice to taste
parsley sprigs to garnish	parsley sprigs to garnish

Joint and skin the chicken (page 65). Clean the giblets and put with the carcass, skin and stock ingredients into a saucepan and simmer gently.

Flour the chicken joints and pat off any excess. Heat the lard in a sauté pan or flameproof casserole until it hazes and fry the chicken joints until golden brown all over. Meanwhile wash the mushrooms, reserve 4–5 for a garnish, and quarter or halve the remainder, or leave whole if small. Remove the chicken from the pan and fry the mushrooms and onion until softened. Draw the pan from the heat and stir in 2–3 tablespoons flour, sufficient to absorb the fat. Gradually blend in the milk, bring to the boil and add 300 ml/½ pint (U.S. 1¼ cups) strained giblet stock. Continue simmering and meanwhile mix together in a cup the tomato purée, paprika, sugar and cream. Blend in 2 tablespoons of the hot sauce and stir into the pan, seasoning to taste with salt and lemon juice. Replace the joints in the sauce, adding stock to cover.

Put on the lid and simmer very gently on top of the stove or in a cool oven (150°C, 300°F, Gas Mark 2) for about 40 minutes or until the chicken legs are tender. Do not allow the sauce to boil as it may separate. Adjust the seasoning.

Serve in a border of fluffy boiled rice. Garnish the border with fried mushroom caps, paprika and parsley sprigs. *Serves 4*

Hungarian chicken paprikash (see above)

Paella a la Valenciana

There are various versions of Paella from the different regions of Spain, but the colourful Valencia dish is the most famous and makes a splendid party piece.

In Spain the huge Mediterranean prawns called *gambas* are used, but fresh or frozen large prawns or scampi may be substituted. Fresh or bottled mussels may be used.

METRIC/IMPERIAL	AMERICAN
1 roasting chicken	1 roaster chicken
parsley, bay leaf and seasoning	parsley, bay leaf and seasoning
3 tablespoons olive oil	$\frac{1}{4}$ cup olive oil
1 large onion, sliced	1 large onion, sliced
1–2 cloves garlic, crushed	1–2 cloves garlic, crushed
350 g/12 oz long-grain rice	1$\frac{3}{4}$ cups long-grain rice
1 large or 2 small red or green	1 large or 2 small red or green
peppers, seeds removed	peppers, seeds removed
1·15 litres/2 pints fresh mussels	5 cups fresh mussels
6 tablespoons dry white wine	$\frac{1}{2}$ cup dry white wine
good pinch powdered saffron	good dash powdered saffron
175 g/6 oz Chorizo or	$\frac{1}{3}$ lb Chorizo or
garlic sausage	garlic sausage
2–3 tablespoons cooked peas	3–4 tablespoons cooked peas
12 large prawns or	12 Dublin Bay prawns or
scampi	jumbo shrimp
lemon wedges to garnish	lemon wedges to garnish

Cut the chicken into six joints and skin (page 65). Boil the carcass, skin and cleaned giblets in water with herbs and seasoning to make stock.

Heat the oil in a paella pan or frying pan and fry the chicken joints until golden all over. Remove the chicken and fry the onion and garlic until softened without colouring, stirring continuously. Add the rice and continue to fry. Put the chicken back and strain in sufficient stock to cover. Simmer over a low heat, adding more stock as it is absorbed and stirring frequently. Slice the peppers thinly and add to the pan. Clean and beard the mussels (page 123) discarding any that are damaged or which float. Put into a saucepan with the wine, cover and cook for 10–15 minutes until the shells open. Lift out the mussels and keep them warm in a folded cloth. Strain the liquor into the rice, add the saffron and stir well. Continue simmering until the rice is tender and the stock absorbed.

Meanwhile, fry the sliced or chopped Chorizo and add to the rice with the cooked peas. Add the prepared prawns or scampi; these will toughen if overcooked. Remove the top shells of the mussels and arrange the bottom halves containing the mussels on the rice. Garnish with lemon wedges. *Serves 6*

Quick chicken liver pâté (see page 78); Maryland chicken (see page 22); Chicken risotto Milanaise (see page 112); Chicken Marengo (see page 88); Savoury pancakes (see page 117) and Petite marmite (see page 61)

Chicken Marengo

(Illustrated on page 86)

This classic dish is reputed to have been invented by Napoleon's army chef to celebrate the victory at Marengo. He had to rely on the surrounding Italian countryside for its ingredients. He garnished it with eggs, deep fried in olive oil, and fresh water crayfish from local streams.

METRIC/IMPERIAL	AMERICAN
1 roasting chicken	1 roaster chicken
1 bay leaf	1 bay leaf
1 sprig parsley	1 sprig parsley
salt and freshly ground black pepper	salt and freshly ground black pepper
2 tablespoons olive oil	3 tablespoons olive oil
25–50 g/1–2 oz butter	2–4 tablespoons butter
flour for coating	flour for coating
2 medium onions, sliced	2 medium onions, sliced
1 clove garlic, crushed	1 clove garlic, crushed
100–225 g/4–8 oz mushrooms	1–2 cups mushrooms
6 tablespoons dry white wine	$\frac{1}{2}$ cup dry white wine
450 g/1 lb ripe tomatoes or 1 (425-g/15-oz) can tomatoes	1 lb ripe tomatoes or 1 (15-oz) can tomatoes
pinch each of dried basil and marjoram	dash each of dried basil and marjoram
salt and freshly ground black pepper	salt and freshly ground black pepper
lemon juice to taste	lemon juice to taste

Joint and skin the chicken (page 65). Clean the giblets (page 54) and put into a saucepan with the carcass, bay leaf, parsley and seasoning and enough cold water to cover. Simmer to make stock.

Heat the oil and butter together in a sauté pan or flameproof casserole. Coat the chicken joints with flour, patting off any surplus, and fry briskly until golden brown all over. Remove from the pan, add the onion, garlic and mushrooms and fry until the onions begin to turn colour. Add the wine and boil for 2–3 minutes. Add the skinned fresh or canned tomatoes, coarsely chopped, the herbs, chicken and sufficient giblet stock to cover the chicken. Bring to the simmer, season to taste with salt, pepper and lemon juice. Cover and cook gently over a low heat for about 40 minutes, or until the legs are tender. Stir well and correct the seasoning before serving with a bowl of rice or pasta. *Serves 4*

Serving suggestions: Arrange the chicken with pasta, such as tagliatelle or rice, garnished with langoustine (crayfish) tails fried in butter. Sprinkle the chicken with chopped fresh parsley and curls of lemon zest.

Arrange the chicken joints in a deep serving dish and garnish with triangles of fried bread topped with buttered spinach purée, flavoured with grated Parmesan cheese.

Chicken breasts Bel Paese

Bel Paese is best for this traditional Italian dish, but another variety which melts easily may be used.

METRIC/IMPERIAL	AMERICAN
4 large chicken breasts	4 large chicken breasts
4 small slices cooked ham	4 small slices cooked ham
4 slices Bel Paese cheese	4 slices Bel Paese cheese
flour for coating	flour for coating
50 g/2 oz butter	$\frac{1}{4}$ cup butter
1 medium onion, thinly sliced	1 medium onion, thinly sliced
4 tomatoes, peeled and sliced	4 tomatoes, peeled and sliced
50 g/2 oz mushrooms, sliced	$\frac{1}{2}$ cup mushrooms, sliced
2 teaspoons finely chopped basil	2 teaspoons finely chopped basil
and/or marjoram or a pinch each	and/or marjoram or a dash each
of the dried varieties	of the dried varieties
1 teaspoon sugar	1 teaspoon sugar
3 tablespoons Marsala or vermouth	$\frac{1}{4}$ cup Marsala or vermouth
150–300 ml/$\frac{1}{4}$–$\frac{1}{2}$ pint stock	$\frac{2}{3}$–1$\frac{1}{4}$ cups chicken stock
salt and freshly ground	salt and freshly ground
black pepper	black pepper
finely chopped basil or parsley	finely chopped basil or parsley
to garnish	to garnish

Fillet the breasts from the bone and open out each one, using the natural separation of the flesh. Cover with greaseproof paper and beat out with a rolling pin or cutlet bat.

Lay a slice of ham on the larger piece of each breast and top with a slice of cheese. Fold over the other half of the breast. Secure with two wooden cocktail sticks. Flatten again and coat with the flour.

Heat the butter in a large flameproof casserole or sauté pan and fry the breasts until browned on both sides. Remove from the pan and fry the onion until soft. Add the tomatoes, mushrooms, herbs and sugar. Cover the pan and cook until the juices run then pour in the Marsala or vermouth. Bring to the boil and add the chicken breasts. Season to taste and simmer gently for about 40 minutes. Alternatively, cook in a cool oven (150°C, 300°F, Gas Mark 2) for the same time.

Remove the chicken and keep warm. Reduce the sauce by brisk boiling until slightly thickened. Return the chicken to the casserole and arrange on a heated serving dish with the sauce, removing the cocktail sticks. Garnish with the chopped basil or parsley. *Serves 4*

Koftas with nut curry sauce

METRIC/IMPERIAL	AMERICAN
3 slices bread	3 slices bread
2 eggs	2 eggs
milk for soaking	milk for soaking
450 g/1 lb chicken meat, minced	1 lb chicken meat, ground
1 teaspoon fennel seed	1 teaspoon fennel seed
1 teaspoon ground cinnamon	1 teaspoon ground cinnamon
$\frac{1}{2}$ teaspoon ground ginger	$\frac{1}{2}$ teaspoon ground ginger
1 small onion, finely chopped	1 small onion, finely chopped
salt and freshly ground black pepper	salt and freshly ground black pepper
breadcrumbs for coating	bread crumbs for coating
deep fat for frying	deep fat for frying

Cut the crusts from the bread and soak the soft part in one of the eggs beaten with a little milk. Mix the chicken with the fennel, cinnamon, ginger and onion. Season well.

Crush the soaked bread with a fork and mix it into the chicken.

With floured fingers, roll the mixture into little balls. Beat the remaining egg and use to coat the balls, then coat the balls in breadcrumbs.

Heat the oil to 190°C/375°F and fry the balls until crisp and golden. Drain on soft paper and serve with the Nut curry sauce (opposite) and fluffy boiled rice.
Serves 4

90

Nut curry sauce

METRIC/IMPERIAL	AMERICAN
2 tablespoons desiccated coconut	3 tablespoons shredded coconut
150 ml/¼ pint boiling water	⅔ cup boiling water
100 g/4 oz cashew nuts	⅔ cup cashew nuts
25 g/1 oz butter or chicken fat	2 tablespoons butter or chicken fat
1 small apple, chopped	1 small apple, chopped
1 small onion, chopped	1 small onion, chopped
1 medium potato, diced	1 medium potato, diced
1 teaspoon curry powder	1 teaspoon curry powder
1 teaspoon curry paste	1 teaspoon curry paste
1 tablespoon flour	1 tablespoon flour
150 ml/¼ pint milk	⅔ cup milk
25 g/1 oz sultanas	3 tablespoons seedless white raisins
salt and freshly ground	salt and freshly ground
black pepper	black pepper
lemon juice to taste	lemon juice to taste

Place the coconut in a bowl and pour on the boiling water. Infuse until required. Roast the nuts until golden under the grill and chop. Melt the butter or fat and fry the apple, onion and potato until just changing colour. Add the curry powder, curry paste and flour and fry for a few minutes.

Strain the liquid from the coconut and stir the infusion into the pan with the milk. Bring to simmering point and add the nuts and sultanas. Simmer until the potato is cooked and the sauce is thick. Season to taste and add lemon juice as liked. Add the kofta balls (opposite) and serve with fluffy boiled rice and cooked poppadums. *Serves 4*

Chinese egg rolls

These make an unusual and tasty starter, or savoury to finish a dinner, or part of a Chinese meal.

METRIC/IMPERIAL	AMERICAN
50 g/2 oz fresh or canned beansprouts	1 cup fresh or canned beansprouts
1 spring onion, finely chopped	1 scallion, finely chopped
50 g/2 oz white button mushrooms, sliced	$\frac{1}{2}$ cup white mushrooms, sliced
1 stick celery heart, chopped	1 stalk celery heart, chopped
1 tablespoon vegetable oil	1 tablespoon vegetable oil
100 g/4 oz cooked chicken meat	$\frac{1}{4}$ lb cooked chicken meat
175–225 g/6–8 oz canned water chestnuts, sliced	1–1$\frac{1}{2}$ cups canned water chestnuts, sliced
1 tablespoon sherry	1 tablespoon sherry
2 teaspoons soy sauce	2 teaspoons soy sauce
2 teaspoons cornflour	2 teaspoons cornstarch
8 thin pancakes	8 thin pancakes
1 egg, beaten	1 egg, beaten
deep fat for frying	deep fat for frying

Trim off and discard any damaged ends from fresh beansprouts. Blanch the beansprouts for 5 minutes in boiling salted water. Drain and chop roughly. If using the canned variety, strain off the liquor and chop as for fresh. Mix together the onion, mushrooms and celery. Heat the oil and fry the vegetable mixture gently until softened. Chop the chicken and add to the pan with the water chestnuts and beansprouts. Fry lightly and stir in the sherry and soy sauce.

Mix the cornflour with 2 (U.S. 3) tablespoons of the liquor from the can of chestnuts. Stir into the pan and continue to cook, stirring until the cornflour is cooked and the other ingredients are well coated.

Spread the pancakes out and spoon the mixture into the centre, dividing it equally between the pancakes. Fold the sides of the pancakes over the filling and seal the edges with the beaten egg. Fold the open ends over to make a neat parcel and seal with beaten egg. Turn upside down and put aside for 20 minutes until set.

Heat the oil to 190°C/375°F with the frying basket in the pan. Fry the rolls a few at a time, without letting them touch each other. Fry until crisp and golden. Drain on soft paper and keep warm while frying the others. *Serves 4*

Sauces for the bird

Blanquette sauce

for boiled bird and vols-au-vent

METRIC/IMPERIAL	AMERICAN
50 g/2 oz butter	$\frac{1}{4}$ cup butter
1 medium onion, thinly sliced	1 medium onion, thinly sliced
2 rashers bacon	2 bacon slices
100 g/4 oz mushrooms, sliced	1 cup sliced mushrooms
1 stick celery, finely chopped	1 stalk celery, finely chopped
2–3 tablespoons flour	3–4 tablespoons flour
300 ml/$\frac{1}{2}$ pint milk	$1\frac{1}{4}$ cups milk
300 ml/$\frac{1}{2}$ pint Chicken stock (page 55)	$1\frac{1}{4}$ cups Chicken stock (page 55)
pinch of grated nutmeg	dash of grated nutmeg
salt and freshly ground white pepper	salt and freshly ground white pepper
lemon juice to taste	lemon juice to taste

Melt the butter in a saucepan and fry the onion, bacon, mushrooms and celery slowly until softened, but not coloured. Draw the pan from the heat and stir in sufficient flour to absorb the fat and make a smooth roux. Gradually blend in the milk and the strained chicken stock. Bring to the simmer and flavour with nutmeg. Season to taste and sharpen with a little lemon juice. Cook gently for 10–15 minutes, stirring frequently.

French onion sauce
Make as a Blanquette sauce, using 2 chopped medium onions and omitting the bacon, mushrooms and celery.

White sauces (Béchamel grasse)

Ordinary white sauce is made with milk added to a roux base of equal quantities of butter and flour, but if the liquid used is half chicken or giblet stock and half milk, a richer, more flavoursome sauce results, which is called Béchamel grasse. It can be used in a number of ways.

Basic béchamel sauce

for coating hot poultry or vegetables

METRIC/IMPERIAL	AMERICAN
50 g/2 oz butter	$\frac{1}{4}$ cup butter
50 g/2 oz flour	$\frac{1}{2}$ cup flour
150 ml/$\frac{1}{4}$ pint milk	$\frac{2}{3}$ cup milk
150 ml/$\frac{1}{4}$ pint Chicken stock	$\frac{2}{3}$ cup Chicken stock
(page 55)	(page 55)
pinch of grated nutmeg	dash of grated nutmeg
salt and freshly ground	salt and freshly ground
white pepper	white pepper

Melt the butter. Draw the pan from the heat and stir in the flour to make a smooth roux. Gradually blend in the milk and then the strained stock. Return to the heat and bring to the boil, beating and stirring continuously to prevent lumps from forming as the sauce thickens. Add the nutmeg and season well with salt and pepper. Cook very gently for 5 minutes or longer, stirring frequently. If the flour is not sufficiently cooked the sauce will taste floury. The finished sauce should cling to the back of a wooden spoon and coat it evenly.

If properly stirred, the sauce will be smooth, but should there be any lumps, they can be easily dispersed with a rotary whisk. Cover to prevent a skin from forming and stand the saucepan in a *bain marie* if it is to be kept warm. Stir before using.

Lemon béchamel sauce
Sharpen the cooked sauce with 2–3 tablespoons fresh lemon juice.

Parsley béchamel sauce
Add 2–3 tablespoons chopped parsley to the cooked sauce.

Cheese béchamel sauce
When the sauce is cooked, draw the pan from the heat and stir in 75–100 g/ 3–4 oz (U. S. $\frac{3}{4}$–1 cup) grated hard cheese. Stir until melted, but do not boil, as the cheese will go stringy.

Egg béchamel sauce
Add 2 chopped hard-boiled eggs to the Parsley or Cheese béchamel sauce.

Panada
This is a thick binding sauce for soufflés, mousses and croquettes. Make as the basic béchamel sauce, but twice as thick by omitting the milk and using only the 150 ml/¼ pint (U. S. ⅔ cup) chicken stock.

Velouté sauce
Beat 2 egg yolks into 3 tablespoons (U. S. scant ¼ cup) cream. Blend in 3 tablespoons béchamel sauce and stir this mixture back into the sauce. Sharpen to taste with lemon juice and cook, stirring, until slightly thickened.

Bread sauce

for roasted and grilled bird

METRIC/IMPERIAL	AMERICAN
1 medium onion	1 medium onion
6–8 cloves	6–8 cloves
about 300 ml/½ pint milk	about 1¼ cups milk
1 bay leaf	1 bay leaf
4–6 slices white bread	4–6 slices white bread
15 g/½ oz butter	1 tablespoon butter
pinch of grated nutmeg	dash of grated nutmeg
salt and freshly ground white pepper	salt and freshly ground white pepper
2–3 tablespoons cream	3–4 tablespoons cream

Peel the onion and spike the bottom with the cloves. Put into a small pan, cloves downwards, and add the milk and bay leaf. Heat very gently to infuse the flavours. Meanwhile, cut the crusts off the bread and dice the slices. When the milk boils, draw the pan off the heat. Add the bread and leave in a warm place for 30 minutes or longer. Do not boil or the bread will become rubbery.

Remove the onion and bay leaf. Add the butter and nutmeg and season well with salt and pepper. Whisk until creamy. If too thick, add a little more milk. Stir in the cream before serving.

Barbecue sauce

for marinating and basting during spit-roasting and grilling

METRIC/IMPERIAL	AMERICAN
1 tablespoon vegetable oil	1 tablespoon vegetable oil
1 medium onion, chopped	1 medium onion, chopped
1 (425-g/15-oz) can tomatoes	1 (15-oz) can tomatoes
3 sticks celery, finely chopped	3 stalks celery, finely chopped
3 tablespoons tarragon vinegar	$\frac{1}{4}$ cup tarragon vinegar
3 tablespoons tomato ketchup	$\frac{1}{4}$ cup tomato ketchup
1 tablespoon Worcestershire sauce	1 tablespoon Worcestershire sauce
1 clove garlic, crushed	1 clove garlic, crushed
3 bay leaves	3 bay leaves
1 tablespoon sugar	1 tablespoon sugar
$\frac{1}{2}$ lemon, thinly sliced	$\frac{1}{2}$ lemon, thinly sliced
300 ml/$\frac{1}{2}$ pint chicken stock	$1\frac{1}{4}$ cups chicken stock
salt and freshly ground black pepper	salt and freshly ground black pepper

Heat the oil and fry the onion slowly until just turning colour. Add the other ingredients and simmer for 20–30 minutes. Remove the bay leaves and lemon slices before using and adjust the seasoning.

Apricot and honey barbecue sauce

This sauce is an attractive alternative for a spitted chicken and is ideal for an indoor barbecue dish, when the chicken is jointed and baked in the oven.

METRIC/IMPERIAL	AMERICAN
1 (425-g/15-oz) can apricot halves	1 (15-oz) can apricot halves
4 teaspoons soy sauce	4 teaspoons soy sauce
4 teaspoons honey	4 teaspoons honey
4 teaspoons tomato ketchup	4 teaspoons tomato ketchup
$\frac{1}{4}$ teaspoon dried rosemary	$\frac{1}{4}$ teaspoon dried rosemary
4 teaspoons lemon juice	4 teaspoons lemon juice
300 ml/$\frac{1}{2}$ pint Chicken stock (page 55)	1$\frac{1}{4}$ cups Chicken stock (page 55)
salt and freshly ground black pepper	salt and freshly ground black pepper
1 chicken, cut in joints	1 chicken, cut in pieces
oil	oil

Strain off the apricot juice and put the fruit into a blender or through a sieve, reserving four halves for garnish. Heat the purée gently in a saucepan with the soy sauce, honey, tomato ketchup and rosemary, until the honey is melted. Sharpen with lemon juice.

Place the chicken joints in an oiled roasting pan and brush with oil. Pour over the sauce and bake for 10 minutes in a hot oven (220°C, 425°F, Gas Mark 7) then turn, baste with the sauce and brown on the other side. Reduce the heat to moderately hot (190°C, 375°F, Gas Mark 5) and continue cooking for a further 20–25 minutes or until tender, basting occasionally.

Remove the chicken to a warm serving dish. Add the stock to the roasting tin and boil up, scraping up the residue from the bottom. Reduce slightly by brisk boiling, adjust the seasoning and pour over the chicken joints. Garnish with the remaining apricot halves. *Serves 4*

Bercy sauce

for boiled or roast bird and hot chicken mousse

METRIC/IMPERIAL	AMERICAN
50 g/2 oz butter	¼ cup butter
1 small onion, finely chopped	1 small onion, finely chopped
6 tablespoons white wine or cider	6 tablespoons white wine or cider
250 ml/8 fl oz Chicken stock	1 cup Chicken stock
(page 55)	(page 55)
1 tablespoon flour	1 tablespoon flour
6 tablespoons cream	½ cup cream
2 teaspoons chopped parsley	2 teaspoons chopped parsley
salt and freshly ground	salt and freshly ground
white pepper	white pepper

Melt half the butter and fry the onion over a low heat until softened. Add the wine and chicken stock and boil, uncovered, until reduced by half.

Make a *beurre manié* by creaming together the remaining butter and the flour. Form the mixture into marble-sized balls. Drop these, one at a time, into the sauce, stirring until it thickens. When it reaches a coating consistency, blend about 5 tablespoons of the sauce into the cream and stir this mixture into the sauce. Add the parsley and season to taste.

White devil sauce

for marinating and basting

METRIC/IMPERIAL	AMERICAN
150 ml/¼ pint double cream	⅔ cup heavy cream
2 tablespoons lemon juice	3 tablespoons lemon juice
2 tablespoons mango chutney	3 tablespoons mango chutney
1 tablespoon mushroom ketchup	1 tablespoon mushroom ketchup
2–3 teaspoons Dijon mustard	2–3 teaspoons Dijon mustard
2 tablespoons soy sauce	3 tablespoons soy sauce
few drops of Tabasco sauce	few drops of Tabasco sauce

Thicken the cream by stirring in the lemon juice. Add all the other ingredients and mix well.

Dark devil sauce

for marinating and basting

METRIC/IMPERIAL	AMERICAN
4 tablespoons tomato ketchup	$\frac{1}{3}$ cup tomato ketchup
2 tablespoons olive oil	3 tablespoons olive oil
2 tablespoons brown pickle sauce	3 tablespoons brown pickle sauce
1 tablespoon cranberry or redcurrant jelly	1 tablespoon cranberry or redcurrant jelly
1 tablespoon tarragon vinegar	1 tablespoon tarragon vinegar
1 tablespoon Worcestershire sauce	1 tablespoon Worcestershire sauce
grated rind and juice of 1 orange	grated rind and juice of 1 orange
salt and freshly ground black pepper	salt and freshly ground black pepper

Mix all the ingredients together, seasoning to taste.

Soured cream and garlic marinade

This is particularly good for frozen chickens. The thawed joints should be covered in the marinade and left for several hours or overnight in the refrigerator. Thick cream may be soured with extra lemon juice or yogurt may be used instead.

METRIC/IMPERIAL	AMERICAN
1 (142-ml/5-fl oz) carton soured cream	1 (5-fl oz) carton dairy sour cream
1 large clove garlic, crushed	1 large clove garlic, crushed
1 tablespoon lemon juice	1 tablespoon lemon juice
1 teaspoon dried thyme or rosemary	1 teaspoon dried thyme or rosemary
1 teaspoon celery salt	1 teaspoon celery salt
$\frac{1}{2}$ teaspoon pepper	$\frac{1}{2}$ teaspoon pepper
$\frac{1}{2}$ teaspoon paprika	$\frac{1}{2}$ teaspoon paprika pepper
$\frac{1}{2}$ teaspoon salt	$\frac{1}{2}$ teaspoon salt

Mix all the ingredients together and use for marinating and basting, during spit-roasting or grilling.

Thick mayonnaise

METRIC/IMPERIAL	AMERICAN
2 egg yolks	2 egg yolks
150 ml/¼ pint olive oil	⅔ cup olive oil
¼ teaspoon salt	¼ teaspoon salt
freshly ground white pepper	freshly ground white pepper
¼ teaspoon French mustard	¼ teaspoon French mustard
(optional)	(optional)
2 teaspoons lemon juice or	2 teaspoons lemon juice or
tarragon vinegar	tarragon vinegar

Put the egg yolks into a basin. Wrap the basin in a cloth to prevent it slipping on the table. Stir with a wooden spoon until creamy. Trickle in the oil, a few drops at a time, stirring steadily in the same direction and at an even speed, until the mayonnaise is quite stiff, when the oil can be added a little faster. Adjust the seasoning and sharpen with lemon juice or tarragon vinegar to taste. *Makes 150 ml/¼ pint (U. S. ⅔ cup)*

Tuna mayonnaise
Pound or sieve a (65-g/2½-oz) can tuna with its oil. Add this to 150 ml/¼ pint (U. S. ⅔ cup) Thick mayonnaise without the mustard. Mix well and sharpen with lemon juice.

Tartare sauce *for cold or grilled bird*
Make 150 ml/¼ pint (U. S. ⅔ cup) Thick mayonnaise, omitting the vinegar. Stir in 2 teaspoons each of finely chopped capers, gherkins, shallots or cocktail onions and 1 tablespoon chopped fresh parsley. Season to taste with mustard and lemon juice.

Gribiche sauce *for cold bird and chicken salad*
Add the sieved yolks of 2 hard-boiled eggs to the raw yolks when making 150 ml/¼ pint (U. S. ⅔ cup) Thick mayonnaise. When the mayonnaise has thickened, stir in the chopped whites of the hard-boiled eggs, 4 teaspoons finely chopped gherkins and 4 teaspoons chopped parsley. Season well and sharpen with tarragon vinegar.

Starters and savouries

Petites royales au Parmesan

A royale is a savoury custard and these are particularly good made with a strong Chicken stock (page 55) or the giblet stock from a roast turkey. When they are set, they are covered with cream and grated cheese and toasted until golden brown on top. These savoury custards can be served as a starter or a savoury.

METRIC/IMPERIAL	AMERICAN
2 whole eggs and 3 egg yolks	2 whole eggs and 3 egg yolks
150 ml/$\frac{1}{4}$ pint double cream	$\frac{2}{3}$ cup heavy cream
450 ml/$\frac{3}{4}$ pint strong Chicken stock (page 55)	2 cups strong Chicken stock (page 55)
1 teaspoon chopped parsley	1 teaspoon chopped parsley
1 teaspoon chopped tarragon	1 teaspoon chopped tarragon
1 teaspoon chopped chives	1 teaspoon chopped chives
salt and freshly ground black pepper	salt and freshly ground black pepper
25 g/1 oz grated Parmesan cheese	$\frac{1}{4}$ cup grated Parmesan cheese
50 g/2 oz Gruyère cheese, grated	$\frac{1}{2}$ cup grated Gruyère cheese

Beat the eggs well together with 2 tablespoons (U. S. 3 tablespoons) cream. Heat the stock slowly with the parsley, tarragon and chives. When it comes to the boil, strain it on to the eggs, stirring vigorously. Season. Butter six dariole moulds or small moulds, about 150 ml/$\frac{1}{4}$ pint (U. S. $\frac{2}{3}$ cup) in size, and fill with the custard.

Put the darioles into a pan with about 2·5 cm/1 inch water in the bottom and simmer gently on top of the stove, or in a *bain marie* in a moderate oven (160°C, 325°F, Gas Mark 3) for 1 hour or until set. Chill well.

Butter a flameproof serving dish or individual shallow bowls. Turn out the royales and pour over the remaining cream. Mix the grated cheeses together and sprinkle generously over the royales. Place in the top of a hot oven (220°C, 425°F, Gas Mark 7) or under a hot grill, until the crust is golden and bubbling. Serve immediately with thin brown bread sandwiches of cress or cucumber.
Serves 6

Pâté de campagne

This French country-style pâté can be made with just chicken or a mixture of poultry and game. The birds can be either part-roasted or boiled, according to age and convenience, until the flesh can be removed and chopped roughly or put through a coarse mincer. If using an electric mincer, be careful to run it only for a few seconds at a time or the traditional rough texture will be lost.

METRIC/IMPERIAL	AMERICAN
100 g/4 oz streaky bacon rashers	¼ lb bacon slices
2 bay leaves	2 bay leaves
450 g/1 lb chicken meat	1 lb chicken meat
100 g/4 oz pickled belly pork	¼ lb salt pork
1 clove garlic, crushed	1 clove garlic, crushed
2 tablespoons chopped parsley	3 tablespoons chopped parsley
pinch of dried thyme	dash of dried thyme
pinch of dried rosemary	dash of dried rosemary
salt and freshly ground black pepper	salt and freshly ground black pepper
1 egg	1 egg
3 tablespoons double cream	¼ cup heavy cream
75–100 g/3–4 oz chicken livers	about ¼ lb chicken livers
40 g/1½ oz butter	3 tablespoons butter
2 tablespoons brandy	3 tablespoons brandy
lemon juice to taste	lemon juice to taste

Remove the rind from the bacon rashers. Lay a bay leaf in the bottom of a 600-ml/1-pint (U.S. 1½-pint) terrine or casserole dish and place one end of the rashers on top of it, radiating out in a star pattern, with the other ends hanging outside the dish. Chop and mince the chicken roughly with the pickled pork. Add the garlic and herbs and season well. Stir in the egg and cream. Divide the chicken livers into neat pieces, removing any discoloured pieces, and sauté quickly in the hot butter until just firm. Pour the surplus butter into the pâté mixture. Warm the brandy in a little pan or a ladle, set alight and pour flaming over the livers. Shake until the flames die out. Set the liver aside and scrape the juices from the pan into the pâté mixture. Sharpen to taste with the lemon juice and adjust the seasoning.

Half-fill the bacon-lined terrine with the pâté mixture and press down. Cover with the sautéed livers. Cover with the remaining minced mixture and fold over the bacon rashers. Place a bay leaf on top. Put on the buttered lid and stand the terrine in a roasting pan with 1 cm/½ inch water in the bottom. Bake in a moderate oven (160°C, 325°F, Gas Mark 3) for 1½ hours or until set.

Allow to chill overnight before cutting, or it will crumble. It can be served in the terrine or turned out. In France, the terrine is served with crusty bread and butter; in England it is usually accompanied with hot toast in a napkin.

Barbecued chicken (see page 16)

Stuffed mushrooms

METRIC/IMPERIAL	AMERICAN
4 very large flat mushrooms	4 very large flat mushrooms
175 g/6 oz cooked chicken meat	6 oz cooked chicken meat
50 g/2 oz butter or margarine	$\frac{1}{4}$ cup butter or margarine
1 small onion, chopped	1 small onion, chopped
2 rashers streaky bacon, chopped	2 bacon slices, chopped
150 ml/$\frac{1}{4}$ pint thick white sauce	$\frac{2}{3}$ cup thick white sauce
50 g/2 oz cheese, grated	$\frac{1}{2}$ cup grated cheese
2 tablespoons finely chopped parsley	3 tablespoons finely chopped parsley
salt and freshly ground black pepper	salt and freshly ground black pepper
few drops Worcestershire sauce or French mustard	few drops Worcestershire sauce or French mustard

Peel the mushroom caps and remove and chop the stalks. Dice the chicken meat. Heat the butter or margarine and fry the onion, bacon and stalks. Remove the mixture from the pan, leaving the butter. Heat the white sauce in a small pan and stir in half the cheese over a low heat. Add the chicken, fried mixture, parsley and seasoning to the sauce and add Worcestershire sauce or French mustard to taste.

Fry the mushrooms on both sides in the butter and arrange in a gratin dish, dark side uppermost. Spoon the hot chicken mixture on to each mushroom and top with the remaining cheese. Place under a hot grill until the cheese is golden and bubbling then serve at once. If it is more convenient, the mushrooms may be filled in advance. When required, finish them off in a hot oven (220°C, 425°F, Gas Mark 7) for 15 minutes or until heated through and nicely browned.
Serves 4

Chicken kebabs (see page 75)

Chicken and almond dip

This can be served as a cocktail savoury or as a first course for lunch or dinner.

METRIC/IMPERIAL	AMERICAN
175 g/6 oz cooked chicken meat, minced	¾ cup cooked chicken meat, ground
100 g/4 oz button mushrooms, minced	1 cup ground mushrooms
2 tablespoons ground almonds	3 tablespoons ground almonds
4 tablespoons Thick mayonnaise (page 100)	⅓ cup Thick mayonnaise (page 100)
4 tablespoons soured cream	⅓ cup dairy sour cream
salt and freshly ground black pepper	salt and freshly ground black pepper
snipped chives and paprika to garnish	snipped chives and paprika pepper to garnish

Mix the dip ingredients together and season to taste. *Makes 600 ml/1 pint (U. S. 2½ cups)*

For cocktails, turn the dip into a large bowl, garnish with prepared vegetables and biscuit dippers.

For a starter, spoon the dip into individual ramekin dishes and garnish. Place each ramekin on a small plate and surround with prepared vegetables and biscuit dippers.

Dippers
Raw cauliflower florets on cocktail sticks.
Tiny button mushrooms on cocktail sticks.
Small sticks of celery head with leaves.
Sticks of raw young carrot, cut with a crinkle chipper.
Small cocktail biscuits or crackers.

Crochette Milanaise

These savoury patties are a favourite way to use up surplus risotto, for a first course or supper dish.

METRIC/IMPERIAL	AMERICAN
1 large or 2 small eggs	1 large or 2 small eggs
about 275 g/10 oz cooked risotto	2 cups cooked risotto
breadcrumbs	bread crumbs
oil or butter	oil or butter

Mix the egg well into the risotto. This should remain a stiff mixture. Take a tablespoon at a time and shape with floured hands into a patty. Coat with crumbs, pressing them well in. Heat the oil or butter and fry the patties until golden, turning once.

Drain on soft paper and serve with watercress tossed in French dressing for a first course, or with buttered spinach for a supper dish. *Serves 4*

Stuffed peppers

Risotto also makes an excellent stuffing for red or green peppers, which are baked and served with tomato sauce as a starter, or lunch or supper dish.

Chicken and pasta salad

METRIC/IMPERIAL	AMERICAN
175 g/6 oz pasta shells or farfella (butterflies)	3 cups pasta shells or farfella (butterflies)
1·75 litres/3 pints water	7½ cups water
3 teaspoons salt	3 teaspoons salt
225–350 g/8–12 oz cooked chicken meat	½–¾ lb cooked chicken meat
1 small celery heart, chopped	1 small celery heart, chopped
½ red pepper, seeds removed and chopped	½ red pepper, seeds removed and chopped
175 g/6 oz cooked peas	1 cup cooked peas
100 g/4 oz button mushrooms, sliced	1 cup button mushrooms, sliced
dressing:	*dressing:*
2 tablespoons cider or wine vinegar	3 tablespoons cider or wine vinegar
¼ teaspoon French mustard	¼ teaspoon French mustard
1 teaspoon castor sugar	1 teaspoon sugar
salt and freshly ground black pepper	salt and freshly ground black pepper
4 tablespoons olive or corn oil	⅓ cup olive or corn oil
1–2 tablespoons crumbled Roquefort or Danish Blue cheese	1–3 tablespoons crumbled Roquefort or Danish Blue cheese

Cook the pasta in the water with the salt for 12 minutes or until just tender. Drain thoroughly in a colander. Chop the chicken and mix with the pasta, celery, pepper, peas and mushrooms.

To make the dressing, mix together the vinegar, mustard, sugar and seasoning. Whisk in the oil and add the cheese, crumbling it up as you add it. Stir into the salad and chill before serving.

This salad can be served in a bowl lined with crisp lettuce leaves for a main course or in individual scallop shells as a starter. *Serves 4–6*

Chicken and ham hash patties

This is a tasty way of using up cold chicken and ham – the proportions can be varied as convenient. It is a good dish for high tea or supper and a favourite on holiday, as it can easily be cooked when camping or sailing.

METRIC/IMPERIAL	AMERICAN
350 g/12 oz cooked chicken meat	¾ lb cooked chicken meat
100 g/4 oz cooked ham	¼ lb cooked ham
450 g/4 oz cooked potato	1 lb cooked potato
2 tablespoons finely chopped parsley	3 tablespoons finely chopped parsley
1 tablespoon Worcestershire sauce or cider vinegar	1 tablespoon Worcestershire sauce or cider vinegar
salt and freshly ground black pepper	salt and freshly ground black pepper
50 g/2 oz butter or margarine	¼ cup butter or margarine
1 large onion, chopped	1 large onion, chopped
1 egg, beaten	1 egg, beaten

Dice the chicken, ham and potato and mix in the parsley and Worcestershire sauce or cider vinegar. Season well. Heat the butter or margarine and fry the onion until just changing colour. Lift from the pan using a slotted spoon and add to the meat mixture. Bind with the egg and adjust the seasoning. Turn on to a lightly floured board and divide into four. Shape into round patties and fry in the fat left in the pan until crisp on both sides. Serve hot. *Serves 4*

Tomatoes stuffed
with chicken and tuna sauce

These stuffed tomatoes make a delicious cold snack. The tomatoes must be firm as well as ripe. If not really large, two per portion may be needed.

METRIC/IMPERIAL	AMERICAN
6 large ripe tomatoes	6 large ripe tomatoes
salt and freshly ground	salt and freshly ground
black pepper	black pepper
100 g/4 oz cooked chicken meat, diced	$\frac{2}{3}$ cup diced cooked chicken meat
Tuna mayonnaise (page 100)	Tuna mayonnaise (page 100)
6 black olives, stoned	6 black olives, pitted

Turn each tomato stem-side downwards and, using a serrated knife, cut off the top. Spoon out all the seeds and core, sprinkle the cases with salt and pepper and turn upside down to drain. Mix the diced chicken with sufficient tuna mayonnaise to bind and fill the tomato cases. Stand them on a serving dish or individual plates. Put the lid back on top of the filling and secure with a cocktail stick topped with a black olive. Garnish with curly endive. *Serves 6.*

Chicken and cream cheese kromeskies

These little savoury puffs are fried crisp and golden. They are served hot, either as a starter or cocktail or dinner savoury, or with tomato sauce as a supper dish.

METRIC/IMPERIAL	AMERICAN
100 g/4 oz cooked chicken meat	$\frac{1}{4}$ lb cooked chicken meat
75 g/3 oz cream cheese	$\frac{3}{4}$ cup cream cheese
2 teaspoons finely chopped onion	2 teaspoons finely chopped onion
2 teaspoons grated Parmesan cheese	2 teaspoons grated Parmesan cheese
salt and paprika	salt and paprika pepper
100 g/4 oz Shortcrust pastry	$\frac{1}{4}$ lb Shortcrust pastry
(page 32)	(page 32)
deep fat for frying	deep fat for frying

Finely chop or mince the chicken and mix with the cream cheese. Add the onion and Parmesan and season with salt and paprika.

Roll the pastry out thinly into a rectangle and cut into 10-cm/4-inch squares. Put a spoonful of filling in the centre of each square. Damp the edges and fold over into a triangle. Press the edges firmly together and mark neatly with the back of a fork. Heat the deep fat to 190°C/380°F and fry the kromeskies a few at a time. When they are puffed, golden and risen to the surface, remove from the fat and drain on soft paper. *Makes 8*

Alternative fillings:
Fill each kromesky with a piece of cooked chicken or chicken liver wrapped in streaky bacon, or with the filling for Chicken and ham pie à la Russe (page 27) or Chicken piroshki (page 35).

Supper dishes and snacks

Chicken risotto Milanaise

(Illustrated on page 86)

Risotto or savoury rice are ideal ways to use the stock, giblets and carcass meat left from a bird which has been jointed for casseroling.

METRIC/IMPERIAL	AMERICAN
2 tablespoons olive oil	3 tablespoons olive oil
1–2 onions, sliced	1–2 onions, sliced
225 g/8 oz long-grain rice	generous 1 cup long-grain rice
about 900 ml/1½ pints Chicken stock (page 55)	about 3¾ cups Chicken stock (page 55)
100 g/4 oz button mushrooms, sliced	1 cup sliced mushrooms
chicken giblets and carcass meat, cooked	chicken giblets and carcass meat, cooked
50 g/2 oz peeled prawns (optional)	2 oz shelled shrimp (optional)
pinch of powdered saffron	dash of powdered saffron
75–100 g/3–4 oz cheese, grated	¾–1 cup grated cheese
paprika and salt to taste	paprika pepper and salt to taste
1–2 roasted peppers to garnish	1–2 roasted peppers to garnish

Heat the oil and fry the sliced onion gently until softened. Stir in the rice (unwashed) and continue frying, stirring continuously until just turning colour. Add sufficient stock to float the rice. Cover and simmer over a low heat until the liquid is absorbed. Add the sliced mushrooms. Continue adding stock as it is absorbed, stirring frequently until the rice is just tender, about 35 minutes. Meanwhile, chop the cooked liver, heart, gizzard and carcass meat coarsely and add to the risotto with the prawns, if used. Stir in just enough saffron to flavour the rice and colour it a delicate yellow. Draw the pan from the heat, stir in the grated cheese and season with paprika and salt.

Cut the peppers in wedges and remove the seeds. Brush with oil and cook on both sides under the grill.

Pile the rice in a warm serving bowl and garnish with the peppers. Serve with a tossed green salad. *Serves 4*

Tagliatelle Tetrazzini

This rich pasta dish was named after the famous opera singer Tetrazzini, who loved good food. It can be made with the flat noodles called tagliatelle or with spaghetti. Serve in individual dishes for a first course or bake in a gratin dish and serve as a lunch or supper dish, with a tossed green salad.

METRIC/IMPERIAL	AMERICAN
225 g/8 oz tagliatelle or spaghetti	½ lb tagliatelle or spaghetti
1·15 litres/2 pints water	5 cups water
2 teaspoons salt	2 teaspoons salt
25 g/1 oz butter	2 tablespoons butter
225 g/8 oz mushrooms, sliced	2 cups sliced mushrooms
300 ml/½ pint Basic béchamel sauce (page 94)	1¼ cups Basic béchamel sauce (page 94)
175 ml/6 fl oz double cream	¾ cup heavy cream
2 tablespoons sherry	3 tablespoons sherry
salt and freshly ground white pepper	salt and freshly ground white pepper
225 g/8 oz cooked chicken meat	½ lb cooked chicken meat
grated Parmesan cheese	grated Parmesan cheese
2 tablespoons flaked almonds	3 tablespoons flaked almonds

Cook the tagliatelle in the boiling salted water for 15 minutes or until just tender and drain in a colander. Meanwhile, melt the butter and fry the mushrooms for 3–5 minutes in a large sauté pan, stirring well. Mix in the drained pasta. Heat the béchamel sauce gently, gradually stirring in the cream. When hot, but not boiling, stir in the sherry and adjust the seasoning. Stir half the sauce into the pasta and mushroom mixture. Add the chopped chicken and add to the remaining sauce.

Turn the pasta mixture into a gratin dish or individual ramekins, hollow out the centre and fill with the chicken mixture. Sprinkle the pasta border with grated Parmesan cheese and the chicken mixture with flaked almonds. Brown in the top of a hot oven (220°C, 425°F, Gas Mark 7) or under the grill. *Serves 4*

Toasted sandwiches

These are hearty savoury snacks for lunch or a fireside supper.

Triple-decker club sandwich

For each sandwich:
Toast 3 slices of bread, remove the crusts and spread with softened butter.
Bottom layer: Cover with sliced chicken, spread with mayonnaise and top with sliced cucumber.
Second layer: Cover with sliced tomato, season well, top with crisply grilled bacon rashers and garnish with leaves of lettuce heart.
Top layer: Press on firmly and secure with four cocktail sticks or toothpicks, each one topped with a stuffed olive.
   Quarter the sandwich when serving.

Toasted double-decker sandwich

For each sandwich:
Toast 2 slices of bread, remove the crusts and spread with softened butter.

Filling 1:
Bottom layer: Cover with sliced cooked chicken and cooked ham. Spread with sweet pickle and top with watercress sprigs.
Top layer: Cover with crumbled Roquefort or Danish Blue cheese and grill until the cheese melts. Place the top on the sandwich.

Filling 2:
Bottom layer: Mix chopped cooked chicken with well-seasoned cream cheese. Spread on toast, sprinkle with chopped salted peanuts and top with garden cress.
Top layer: Cover with sliced tomatoes, season with salt, pepper and sugar and grill until just colouring. Place the top on the sandwich and garnish with parsley.

Filling 3:
Bottom layer: Cover with sliced cooked chicken, spread with mango or apricot chutney.
Top layer: Top with crumbled Cheshire cheese and grill until the cheese melts. Place the top on the sandwich and garnish with parsley.

Fried sandwiches

Remove the crusts from the bread slices and spread with softened butter. Cover the bottom slice with the chosen filling, press the top slice firmly on top and cut into fingers. Shallow fry in hot butter or lard until crisp and golden, turning once. Drain on soft paper and serve at once.

Filling 1:
Sliced cooked chicken, spread with sweet pickle and topped with sliced Bel Paese or Gouda cheese.

Filling 2:
Chopped cooked chicken and diced ham bound with thick cold Cheese béchamel sauce (page 94).

Cheesy chicken à la King

METRIC/IMPERIAL	AMERICAN
1½ cups Cheese béchamel sauce (page 94)	1½ cups Cheese béchamel sauce (page 94)
1½ cups diced cooked chicken	1½ cups diced cooked chicken
½ cup chopped canned pimientos	½ cup chopped canned pimientos
½ cup canned button mushrooms	½ cup canned button mushrooms
1 egg yolk	1 egg yolk
1 tablespoon sherry	1 tablespoon sherry
salt and freshly ground black pepper	salt and freshly ground black pepper
slices of bread	slices of bread
3–4 tablespoons flaked almonds	4–5 tablespoons flaked almonds

Warm the sauce over a gentle heat, stirring continuously. Mix in the chicken and pimiento. Halve the mushrooms and add. Mix 2 tablespoons of the sauce with the beaten egg yolk, then stir into the pan. Heat the sauce until thickened, but do not boil. Flavour with sherry and season to taste.

Toast one slice of bread for each serving. Remove the crusts, cover with the chicken mixture and sprinkle with flaked almonds which have been toasted under the grill until crisp and golden.

Cheesy chicken à la King makes a tasty filling for vols-au-vent (page 29) and Savoury pancakes (page 117). *Serves 4–6*

Cold French omelette

METRIC/IMPERIAL	AMERICAN
4 eggs	4 eggs
15 g/½ oz butter	1 tablespoon butter
150 ml/¼ pint Cheese béchamel sauce (page 94)	⅔ cup Cheese béchamel sauce (page 94)
100 g/4 oz cooked chicken meat, diced	⅔ cup diced cooked chicken meat
1 tablespoon chopped parsley	1 tablespoon chopped parsley
1 teaspoon chopped chives or tarragon	1 teaspoon chopped chives or tarragon
salt and freshly ground black pepper	salt and freshly ground black pepper
watercress to garnish	watercress to garnish

Make a large omelette with the eggs and butter in a frying pan. When just cooked, do not fold, but slide flat on to a large plate and leave to cool.

Mix the sauce with the chicken and herbs. Season to taste. Spread this filling over the omelette and roll up. Serve cold, garnished with watercress. Accompany with French bread and butter. *Serves 2–3*

Savoury pancakes

(Illustrated on page 86)

METRIC/IMPERIAL	AMERICAN
4 large or 8 small thin pancakes	4 large or 8 small thin pancakes
50 g/2 oz butter or margarine	$\frac{1}{4}$ cup butter or margarine
50 g/2 oz button mushrooms	$\frac{1}{2}$ cup mushrooms
1 small onion, chopped	1 small onion, chopped
50 g/2 oz flour	$\frac{1}{2}$ cup flour
150 ml/$\frac{1}{4}$ pint milk	$\frac{2}{3}$ cup milk
150 ml/$\frac{1}{4}$ pint Chicken stock	$\frac{2}{3}$ cup Chicken stock
(page 55)	(page 55)
100 g/4 oz hard cheese, grated	1 cup grated hard cheese
salt and freshly ground	salt and freshly ground
black pepper	black pepper
350 g/12 oz cooked chicken meat	$\frac{3}{4}$ lb cooked chicken meat
50 g/2 oz frozen prawns (optional)	$\frac{1}{2}$ cup frozen shrimp (optional)
melted butter for brushing	melted butter for brushing
fried mushrooms and parsley	fried mushrooms and parsley
to garnish	to garnish

Make the pancakes and set aside. Heat the butter in a saucepan and fry the mushrooms and onion until soft. Remove the pan from the heat and stir in the flour to absorb the fat. Gradually stir in the milk. Return the pan to the heat and cook, stirring, until thickened. Add the stock and stir well. Simmer for 5 minutes. Remove from the heat, stir in three-quarters of the cheese and season to taste. If liked set aside a few spoonsful of the sauce for a topping. Cut the chicken into dice and add to the sauce with the prawns if used.

Divide the filling between the pancakes, placing it down the centre of each pancake. Fold over the sides of the pancakes and arrange in a buttered gratin dish in a single layer. Brush the pancakes with melted butter and top with the sauce and reserved cheese. Heat through in a moderately hot oven (200°C, 400°F, Gas Mark 6) for about 15 minutes, or until crisp on top. Serve garnished with fried mushrooms and parsley. Alternatively, omit the sauce topping, brush with melted butter and sprinkle generously with grated cheese. Heat through until crisp on top. *Serves 4*

Hot chicken mousse with Bercy sauce

This is a tasty light dish to tempt delicate appetites. It is made like a soufflé, but because it is steam-baked, it will await the guests' pleasure without collapsing, which makes life easier for many an anxious hostess. A French onion sauce (page 93) may be served instead of the Bercy sauce.

METRIC/IMPERIAL	AMERICAN
350 g/12 oz cooked chicken meat	¾ lb cooked chicken meat
oil	oil
2–3 tablespoons crisp	3–4 tablespoons crisp
breadcrumbs	bread crumbs
25 g/1 oz butter	2 tablespoons butter
25 g/1 oz flour	¼ cup flour
4 tablespoons milk	⅓ cup milk
4 tablespoons Chicken stock	⅓ cup Chicken stock
(page 55)	(page 55)
2 eggs, separated	2 eggs, separated
5 tablespoons cream	6 tablespoons cream
1 tablespoon chopped parsley	1 tablespoon chopped parsley
pinch of dried lemon thyme	dash of dried lemon thyme
2 teaspoons mushroom or	2 teaspoons mushroom or
tomato ketchup	tomato ketchup
salt and freshly ground	salt and freshly ground
black pepper	black pepper
1 tablespoon lemon juice	1 tablespoon lemon juice
300 ml/½ pint Bercy sauce	1¼ cups Bercy sauce
(page 98)	(page 98)
lemon and parsley to garnish	lemon and parsley to garnish

Mince the chicken meat very finely.

Oil a cake tin or 1-litre/1½-pint (U. S. 2-pint) charlotte mould. Put in the crisp crumbs and rotate the tin carefully so that the bottom and sides are evenly coated with crumbs. Turn the tin upside down to tip out any loose crumbs.

Heat the oven to moderate (160°C, 325°F, Gas Mark 3). To make a panada, melt the butter, remove the pan from the heat and blend in the flour and then the milk and the stock. Return to the heat and bring to the simmer, stirring continuously. Cook for 3 minutes into a thick binding sauce.

Mix in the minced chicken. Beat the egg yolks and cream together and stir this into the mixture. Add the parsley, lemon thyme and ketchup. Season well, using plenty of freshly ground black pepper. Sharpen with lemon juice.

Whisk the whites until stiff, but not brittle. Turn the mixture into a mixing bowl and carefully fold in the egg whites. Pour into the prepared mould and cover with greased paper. Stand the mould in a roasting pan with 1 cm/½ inch water in the bottom. Bake for about 1 hour or until set. Test by pressing the top with the fingers, it will feel springy when the mousse is ready. Allow to shrink slightly from the sides of the tin, then turn out on to a warm serving dish. Garnish with lemon and parsley and hand Bercy sauce separately or, if preferred, coat with the sauce. Instead of turning it out, the mousse can be cooked and served in a soufflé dish. If made in individual ramekins, they will be cooked in half the time. *Serves 4*

Baked savoury potatoes

Baked jacket potatoes are always popular and, with this savoury filling of chicken and mushrooms, make a super supper snack for the garden in summer, or by the fireside in winter.

METRIC/IMPERIAL	AMERICAN
4 large potatoes	4 large potatoes
vegetable oil	vegetable oil
50 g/2 oz mushrooms, sliced	½ cup sliced mushrooms
100 g/4 oz butter	½ cup butter
100 g/4 oz cooked chicken meat, diced	⅔ cup diced cooked chicken meat
1 (142-ml/5-fl oz) carton soured cream	1 (5-fl oz) carton dairy sour cream
1 tablespoon snipped chives	1 tablespoon snipped chives
salt and freshly ground black pepper	salt and freshly ground black pepper
3–4 tablespoons milk	4–5 tablespoons milk
4 tablespoons grated cheese	⅓ cup grated cheese
few sprigs parsley to garnish	few sprigs parsley to garnish

Scrub the potatoes and halve lengthways. Brush the cut surface with vegetable oil and place cut side down on an oiled baking tray. Prick over the skin with a fork. Bake in a hot oven (220°C, 425°F, Gas Mark 7) for 35–40 minutes or until cooked, according to size.

Meanwhile, heat 2 tablespoons (U.S. 3 tablespoons) butter and fry the mushrooms for 3 minutes. Add the chicken, soured cream and chives and heat through. Season with salt and freshly ground black pepper.

Remove the potatoes from the oven and scoop out the pulp. Mash with the remaining butter and add sufficient milk to make a creamy consistency. Season well. Half fill the skins with the potato purée and hollow out the centre. Spoon in the chicken mixture, cover with the remaining potato, forking it over roughly. Sprinkle with grated cheese and return to the oven until golden. Garnish with parsley. *Serves 4*

Stuffings for the bird

Almond and chicken liver stuffing

for poussins and small chickens

METRIC/IMPERIAL	AMERICAN
1 chicken liver	1 chicken liver
50 g/2 oz rice, boiled	$\frac{1}{3}$ cup rice, boiled
25 g/1 oz ground almonds	$\frac{1}{4}$ cup ground almonds
4 teaspoons finely chopped onion	4 teaspoons finely chopped onion
4 teaspoons chopped parsley	4 teaspoons chopped parsley
pinch of dried basil or	dash of dried basil or
marjoram	marjoram
salt and freshly ground	salt and freshly ground
black pepper	black pepper
50 g/2 oz butter, creamed	$\frac{1}{4}$ cup butter, creamed
1 egg yolk	1 egg yolk

Mash the liver with a fork and mix into the rice with the other dry ingredients and seasonings. Beat in the creamed butter and bind with the egg yolk.

Rice and watercress stuffing

for chicken and game birds

METRIC/IMPERIAL	AMERICAN
50 g/2 oz rice, boiled	$\frac{1}{3}$ cup rice, boiled
1 bunch watercress, finely chopped	1 bunch watercress, finely chopped
2 tablespoons finely chopped celery	3 tablespoons finely chopped celery
1 tablespoon finely chopped onion	1 tablespoon finely chopped onion
1 teaspoon salt	1 teaspoon salt
freshly ground black pepper	freshly ground black pepper
to taste	to taste
1 chicken liver, cleaned	1 chicken liver, cleaned
50 g/2 oz butter, melted	$\frac{1}{4}$ cup melted butter
1 small egg, beaten	1 small egg, beaten

Mix together the drained rice, watercress, celery and onion. Season well with salt and pepper. Chop the chicken liver, or mash with a fork, and stir it into the mixture. Mix in the butter and bind with the egg.

Apple, apricot and nut stuffing

for chicken, pheasant and guinea fowl

METRIC/IMPERIAL	AMERICAN
50 g/2 oz cashew nuts	$\frac{1}{3}$ cup cashew nuts
40 g/1$\frac{1}{2}$ oz butter	3 tablespoons butter
3 tablespoons finely chopped celery	$\frac{1}{4}$ cup finely chopped celery
1 tablespoon finely chopped onion	1 tablespoon finely chopped onion
75 g/3 oz apple, diced	$\frac{1}{2}$ cup diced apple
50 g/2 oz white bread, diced	1 cup diced white bread
75 g/3 oz dried apricots, chopped	$\frac{1}{2}$ cup chopped dried apricots
$\frac{1}{2}$ teaspoon dried savory or rosemary	$\frac{1}{2}$ teaspoon dried savory or rosemary
salt and freshly ground black pepper	salt and freshly ground black pepper
lemon juice to taste	lemon juice to taste

Chop the nuts coarsely. Melt the butter in a small saucepan and fry the nuts until just colouring. Add the celery, onion and apple, fry gently until slightly softened. Mix in the bread, apricots, herbs and seasoning. Stir until well mashed together. Sharpen to taste with lemon juice.

Farce for galantine of chicken

METRIC/IMPERIAL

225 g/8 oz lean pork, minced
100 g/4 oz veal, minced
100 g/4 oz ham, chopped
100 g/4 oz button mushrooms, chopped
1 chicken liver
25 g/1 oz butter
1–2 tablespoons brandy
2 shallots, chopped or 1 clove garlic, crushed
1 tablespoon chopped parsley
grated rind of $\frac{1}{2}$ lemon
salt and freshly ground black pepper
1 egg, beaten

AMERICAN

$\frac{1}{2}$ lb lean pork, ground
$\frac{1}{4}$ lb veal, ground
$\frac{1}{2}$ cup chopped cooked ham
1 cup chopped mushrooms
1 chicken liver
2 tablespoons butter
1–3 tablespoons brandy
2 shallots, chopped or 1 clove garlic, crushed
1 tablespoon chopped parsley
grated rind of $\frac{1}{2}$ lemon
salt and freshly ground black pepper
1 egg, beaten

Work together the pork, veal, ham and mushrooms. Clean the chicken liver. Heat the butter and fry the liver for a few minutes until stiffened. Chop and add to the minced meat. Pour the brandy into the frying pan, boil up and add to the farce. Add the onion or garlic, parsley and lemon rind. Season well with salt and pepper. Mix thoroughly and bind with the beaten egg.

Preparation and serving suggestions

To make hot French garlic bread

Slash a long French loaf across in slices 2·5–3 cm/1–1¼ inches wide, without cutting right through. Crush a large clove of garlic into 100 g/4 oz (U. S. ½ cup) butter. Spread this mixture generously between the slices. Wrap the loaf in aluminium foil and bake in a moderately hot oven (200°C, 400°F, Gas Mark 6) for about 10 minutes.

The preparation and cleaning of mussels

Throughout cleaning, keep the mussels in cold water. Discard any with broken shells, any that are gaping open and any in which the two shells can be slid against each other – the latter will be full of sand and will make the others gritty. With a sharp knife, remove the beard or seaweed-like bits protruding from the shell, scrape off any barnacles or limpets. Scrub the shells and wash them in several waters until finally the water comes out quite free from grit.

Vegetable recipe suggestions

Corn on the cob Indian-style: Turn back the husks and strip off the silky threads. Fold over the husks again so the kernel is covered by the leaves. Roast over a charcoal brazier, turning frequently, for 15–20 minutes. To serve, remove the husks, spread the corn with butter and serve with salt and freshly ground pepper.

Corn fritters: Add 6 tablespoons (U. S. ½ cup) self-raising flour to 1 (227-g/8-oz) can corn kernels and mix in 2 beaten eggs. Heat some butter and oil in a frying pan and drop the batter in by the tablespoonful. Fry until golden brown, turn and fry on the other side. Serve immediately.

Courgettes au gratin: Wipe the courgettes, remove the stalks and halve lengthways. In a shallow flameproof casserole, fry the cut surfaces in hot butter. Turn over, season well and sprinkle with grated Parmesan cheese. Cover and bake in a moderate oven (180°C, 350°F, Gas Mark 4) for 20–30 minutes, according to size. When serving, pour over a little warmed cream.

Jacket potatoes: Prick the potatoes and brush with oil. Bake in a hot oven (220°C, 425°F, Gas Mark 7) for 1 hour or longer, according to size. When cooked, cut a cross in the top, squeeze up the flesh and fork in parsley butter, soured cream and chopped chives or crisp bacon bits. Serve in folded coloured napkins.

Spinach croquettes: Add 50 g/2 oz (U.S. ½ cup) grated Parmesan cheese to 350 g/12 oz (U.S. ¾ lb) cooked, drained and chopped spinach. Season with nutmeg, salt and pepper and beat in 2 egg yolks. Form the mixture into small croquettes on a floured board. Roll them in breadcrumbs and fry in hot butter.

Index

126

127